T0207145

Azure Virtual Desktop Specialist

Exam Study Guide - AZ-140

Shabaz Darr

Apress®

Azure Virtual Desktop Specialist: Exam Study Guide - AZ-140

Shabaz Darr
Bradford, UK

ISBN-13 (pbk): 978-1-4842-7986-1   ISBN-13 (electronic): 978-1-4842-7987-8
https://doi.org/10.1007/978-1-4842-7987-8

Managing Director, Apress Media LLC: Welmoed Spahr
Acquisitions Editor: Smriti Srivastava
Development Editor: Laura Berendson
Coordinating Editor: Shrikant Vishwakarma
Copy Editor: Kezia Endsley

Cover designed by eStudioCalamar

Cover image designed by Pexels

Distributed to the book trade worldwide by Springer Science+Business Media LLC, 1 New York Plaza, Suite 4600, New York, NY 10004. Phone 1-800-SPRINGER, fax (201) 348-4505, e-mail orders-ny@springer-sbm. com, or visit www.springeronline.com. Apress Media, LLC is a California LLC and the sole member (owner) is Springer Science + Business Media Finance Inc (SSBM Finance Inc). SSBM Finance Inc is a **Delaware** corporation.

For information on translations, please e-mail booktranslations@springernature.com; for reprint, paperback, or audio rights, please e-mail bookpermissions@springernature.com, or visit http://www.apress.com/ rights-permissions.

Apress titles may be purchased in bulk for academic, corporate, or promotional use. eBook versions and licenses are also available for most titles. For more information, reference our Print and eBook Bulk Sales web page at http://www.apress.com/bulk-sales.

Any source code or other supplementary material referenced by the author in this book is available to readers on GitHub via the book's product page, located at https://link.springer.com/book/10.1007/978-1-4842-7986-1.

Printed on acid-free paper

This book is dedicated to a few people. To my mother, for being my biggest supporter; and to my late father, for always giving me the best advice, which has allowed me to grow into the person I am today. To my amazing wife Reema for being my rock; this would not be possible without her support. Finally, to my two amazing children, Zoya and Mikaeel, for keeping me sane and for making me smile.

Table of Contents

About the Author

Shabaz Darr has more than 15 years of experience in the IT industry and more than eight years working with cloud technologies. Currently, he works as a Infrastructure Master for Netcompany. He is a certified Microsoft MVP in Enterprise Mobility and a certified Microsoft trainer with certifications in Azure Virtual Desktop Administrator, Office 365 Identity and Services, Modern Workplace Administrator Associate, and Azure Administrator Associate.

About the Technical Reviewer

 **Bhadresh Shiyal** is an Azure data architect and an Azure data engineer. For the past seven and a half years, he has worked with a big IT multi-national corporation as a solutions architect. Prior to that, he spent almost a decade in private and public sector banks in India in various IT positions, working on various Microsoft technologies. He has 20 years of IT experience, two years of which he worked on an international assignment in London. He has very rich experiences in application design, development, and deployment.

He has worked on Visual Basic, SQL Server, SharePoint technologies, .NET MVC, O365, Azure Data Factory, Azure Databricks, Azure Synapse Analytics, Azure Data Lake Storage Gen1/Gen2, Azure SQL Data Warehouse, Power BI, Spark SQL, Scala, Delta Lake, Azure Machine Learning, Azure Information Protection, Azure .NET SDK, Azure DevOps, and more.

He holds multiple Azure certifications, including Microsoft Certified Azure Solutions Architect Expert, Microsoft Certified Azure Data Engineer Associate, Microsoft Certified Azure Data Scientist Associate, and Microsoft Certified Azure Data Analyst Associate.

He worked as a solutions architect on large-scale Azure Data Lake implementation and data transformation projects using Azure Databricks and Azure Synapse Analytics, along with large-scale customized content management systems. He also authored a book titled *Beginning Azure Synapse Analytics* and was the technical reviewer on *Data Science Using Azure* and *Design and Deploy Microsoft Azure Virtual Desktop.*

Acknowledgments

Writing a book has been one of the toughest projects I have completed and it is something I am very proud of. It would not be possible without the help, love, and support of several people. The support of my family is unmeasurable, especially of my wife, Reema. Writing a book of this size and detail is very time-consuming, and her support, motivation, and love helped me along the journey. Without her, this book would not be possible. I also have to mention my two children, Zoya and Mikaeel, who have been my inspiration throughout this project. They made me laugh and smile on those tough days when my motivation was lacking.

I will always be grateful to my parents for making sacrifices and supporting me throughout my life and career. To my siblings, Shazia, Jawwad, Sobia, and Sadia, for always keeping me grounded.

My final acknowledgements are to the Cloud community, which is like a second family to me and has been very supportive since I started this journey. There are too many people to mention, but I will always be grateful for their support and friendship.

Introduction

This book is an exam study guide based on the Microsoft Azure Virtual Desktop Specialist certification. Each chapter of the book covers a section of the official Microsoft exam and includes lab exercises to help you gain practical skills as well as theoretical knowledge about Azure Virtual Desktop.

This book is for IT professionals who want to complete the Azure Virtual Desktop Specialist exam or who want to learn how to administer Azure Virtual Desktop. The book is broken into six chapters, which cover the different elements covered on the exam.

- Chapter 1 explains what Azure Virtual Desktop is from a high level and explains the different ways to schedule and take the Azure Virtual Desktop Specialist exam. It also mentions some links to free resources that you can use in addition to this book that will help you prepare for the exam.

- Chapter 2 takes a deep look into planning an Azure Virtual Desktop deployment, including prerequisites you need, how to design the architecture, and what you need in order to design the user profile element for Azure Virtual Desktop.

- Chapter 3 focuses on implementation. Once you have completed this chapter, you will understand how to implement and manage Azure networking and storage for Azure Virtual Desktop, configure hostpools and sessions hosts, and be able to create and manage session host images.

- Chapter 4 covers managing access and security to Azure Virtual Desktop. After completing this chapter, you will understand how to manage access, including role-based access control (RBAC), managing roles, and configuring restrictions to Azure Virtual Desktop. You will also be able to manage security on Azure Virtual Desktop, including managing policies with conditional access, implementing multi-factor authentication (MFA), and managing security using Azure Security Center.

- Chapter 5 moves onto managing user environments and applications for Azure Virtual Desktop. This chapter focuses on implementing and managing FSLogix for user profiles, configuring the user experience, and the different ways that you can install and configure applications on session hosts.

- Chapter 6 is the final chapter of the book. It covers monitoring and maintenance aspects of Azure Virtual Desktop. In this chapter, you learn how to automate management tasks in Azure Virtual Desktop and how to manage and monitor performance and health.

CHAPTER 1

Exam Overview and Introduction to Azure Virtual Desktop

You are starting your journey with Microsoft role-based certifications. The "Configuring and Operating Microsoft Azure Virtual Desktop" exam is based on Azure Virtual Desktop. This chapter provides direction on getting equipped for the Microsoft exam, as well as outlining resources that can aide you during your learning journey. It provides useful links and explains how you can obtain access to Microsoft 365 and Azure subscriptions on a trial basis, which allow you to gain hands-on experience. This chapter gives you the understanding and knowledge you need to prepare for the exam and become an Azure Virtual Desktop administrator.

This chapter covers the following main topics:

- Preparing for a Microsoft exam

- Accessing resources and Microsoft Learn

- Creating a Microsoft 365 and Azure trial account

- Introducing the AZ-140 exam objectives

- Explaining why you should take this exam

- Introducing Azure Virtual Desktop

© Shabaz Darr 2022
S. Darr, *Azure Virtual Desktop Specialist*, https://doi.org/10.1007/978-1-4842-7987-8_1

Technical Requirements

To complete the exercises in this book, you need access to a Microsoft 365 tenant. This can be attained by signing up for a trial subscription. Additionally, Azure Virtual Desktop services require one of the following licenses:

- Microsoft 365 Business Premium

- Microsoft 365 E5/E3

- Microsoft 365 A3/A5/Student Benefits

- Microsoft 365 F3

- Windows 10 Enterprise E3/E5

- Windows 10 Education A3/A5

- Windows 10 VDA per user

Preparing for a Microsoft Exam

There are several parts to preparing for a Microsoft exam, including accessing the appropriate resources, being able to access a subscription for the hands-on labs, and determining the method by which you are going to take the exam. Understanding the format of Microsoft exams is vitally important, especially if this is your first exam.

Accessing Resources to Prepare for the Exam

You can find multiple resources to help you prepare for Microsoft exams. These include online video content from learning companies, live tutorials from Microsoft Learning Partners, and content from members of the wider community and Microsoft blog articles. All these resources are helpful, but the video content from learning companies and live courses are not free and may not be within your budget. Microsoft blog articles and community-based content can provide you with a route you can follow for each topic, but they do not go into enough detail to fully cover the scope of the certification.

Microsoft provides one of the best resources available. You can find documentation on all services within Microsoft docs, which enables you to search and find the information you need. The information is all public and free, and Microsoft docs are very closely tied to the Microsoft Learn content.

You can access and search Microsoft docs by going to the following link: `https://docs.microsoft.com`.

Accessing a Microsoft 365 Subscription

It is highly recommended that you get hands-on experience with the services in the objectives as part of your preparation. Microsoft courses have GitHub repositories for labs that are publicly available and free.

Guides for the labs can be found at the following link: `https://github.com/MicrosoftLearning/AZ-140-Configuring-and-Operating-Microsoft-Azure-Virtual-Desktop`.

You can take advantage of Microsoft trial subscriptions for both Azure and Microsoft 365. We provide further information on setting up a trial subscription later in this chapter.

Exam Locations

One of the key elements of the exam-preparation process is taking your exam. Traditionally, there has only ever been one option—you take the exams at a proctored exam site. Some people still prefer this method, as it is a controlled environment. Ensuring that you understand the setup of the location where you are taking the exam can be helpful, thus minimizing the level of stress and allowing you to focus on the actual exam.

In more recent times, roughly when role-based exams were made available, Microsoft has provided the option of taking online-proctored exams. These setups allow you to take the exam from home or work, rather than going to an authorized exam site. Some people prefer this option, as it allows them to utilize their own equipment and environment. Note that the online-proctored option is not available in all regions; however, if it is available in your region, you will see something similar to Figure 1-1 when selecting your location.

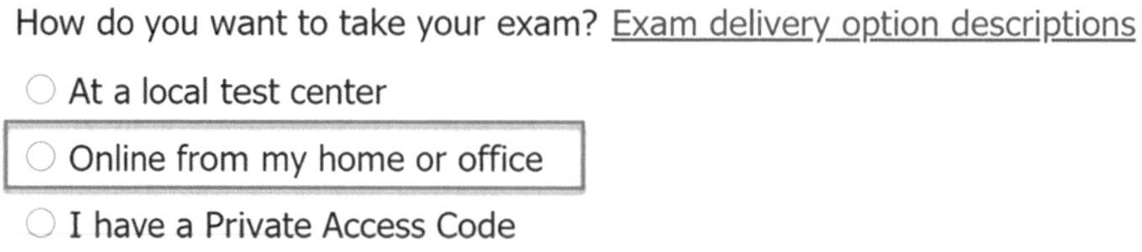

How do you want to take your exam? <u>Exam delivery option descriptions</u>

○ At a local test center

○ Online from my home or office

○ I have a Private Access Code

Figure 1-1. *Location selection when scheduling the exam*

Preparing for the online-proctored exam is much different from preparing for a local test center exam. In relation to the physical equipment, you must have a device with speakers, a microphone, and a webcam. You are only permitted to use a single monitor, so be sure to have a high-resolution monitor to avoid any issues with visibility.

Testing the equipment in advance of taking the exam is highly recommended, as this will allow you to avoid any delays on exam day. You must ensure the environment in which you are taking the exam is clear of any papers, books, pens, and pencils. It must also be an area that is quiet and isolated; no one can enter while you are taking the exam.

Before starting the exam, you will be asked to provide photos of the surrounding area to the left and right sides, as well as the front and back. A valid photo identification (such as a passport or driver's license) is required as well. You must also remain in the view of the camera for the duration of the exam.

Microsoft Exam Format

All Microsoft exams are made up of four to six question types—multiple choice, drag and drop, true/false, drop-down, best answer scenarios, and case studies. The following list describes these question types in detail:

- **Multiple Choice** type questions are straightforward. A question may have more than one answer. The exam questions mention how many correct answers you need to choose for each question, and you will be alerted if you select the incorrect number of choices.

- **Drag and Drop** type questions are typically based on actions of a process and they test your understanding of the order of operations to configure a service. There are more potential answers given than you need, and you are required to move the steps that are appropriate to the question over to the right side in the correct sequence.

- **True/False** questions are slightly different from traditional questions. You are usually provided screenshots from the relevant Microsoft Portals that show you what has been configured. You will then find three to four options, based on whether the statements are correct given the information provided.

- **Drop-down** questions are typically the ones with PowerShell or Azure CLI code in them. You are asked to achieve certain steps within a string of code, where the blank sections provide the drop-down selections to choose from.

- **Best answer scenario** type questions are used to test genuine understanding of an objective. You receive a warning when you get to this section that states you are unable to scroll backwards in these questions. The question provides a specific scenario that needs to be solved, along with a potential solution. You must establish whether the solution is the best one to solve the scenario. You can select yes or no, after which you get the same scenario but with a different possible solution, to which you must again select yes or no.

- **Case study** type questions provide a fictitious company setting with an existing environment, future environment, and business and technical requirements. You are then asked multiple (five-seven) questions that cover multiple objective areas of the exam. You will find one to three case study type questions on the associate level exam.

These various question types test your level of understanding in different ways, and they all go into the weighted exam goals discussed later in this chapter.

So far, we have covered the exam question types as well as the different ways you can sit for the exam. The following sections cover the various resources that will aide you in the process of learning the topics covered on the AZ-140 exam. This chapter also discusses how to gain access to the solutions, which enable you to follow along with the exercises in this book.

Accessing Resources and Microsoft Learn

Microsoft Learn is a good resource for studying for the exam. One of the major benefits of this content is that it is free. When you create a Microsoft account, you can track your progress and acquire badges along your journey. Microsoft also creates learning challenges with intermittent prizes, such as free exam vouchers. You can create a free account by selecting Sign In at the top-right side of the page, as shown in Figure 1-2.

Figure 1-2. *Microsoft Learn sign-in*

You have the option of signing in with an existing Microsoft account or of creating one to get access to the content, as shown in Figure 1-3.

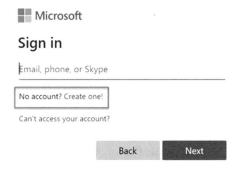

Figure 1-3. *Sign in or create a new Microsoft account*

To access the Microsoft Learn content, use the following link: `https://www.microsoft.com/learn`.

Relevant content can be found on Microsoft Learn in many ways. You can search for specific roles, products, or certification codes. You can find these options on the selection ribbon at the top of the Learn page, as shown in Figure 1-4. You can also find several recommendations for starting on the same page.

Figure 1-4. *Microsoft Learn navigation*

You can select the drop-down arrows from the Learn site's navigation tabs to filter for content in the specific Roles, Products, or Certifications, as shown in Figure 1-5.

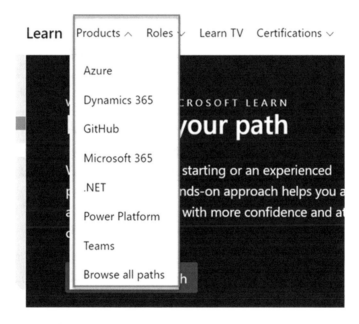

Figure 1-5. *Category filter drop-down arrow*

After you choose the subject that you want to learn about, you can search on a specific topic within that subject. You can filter even further on particular topics or individual courses and even on learning paths, as shown in Figure 1-6.

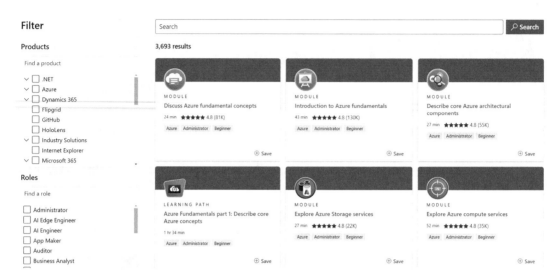

Figure 1-6. *Microsoft Learn content library*

This section looked at the information needed to access the Microsoft Learn content library and showed you how to browse for learning modules and learning paths. The next section guides you through finding content that is particular to the AZ-140 exam.

Microsoft Exam Information Pages

An additional common area on the Microsoft Learn site are the exam pages. There is an exam page for every Microsoft exam, as well as a general certification page. These pages deliver an overview of the exam certification, the objectives of the exam, the roles of individuals that may be interested in the exam, information about scheduling the exam, and the learning path to prepare for the exam. These pages are very helpful when you are studying for a specific exam, rather than just learning general technical knowledge. Figure 1-7 shows the AZ-140 exam search.

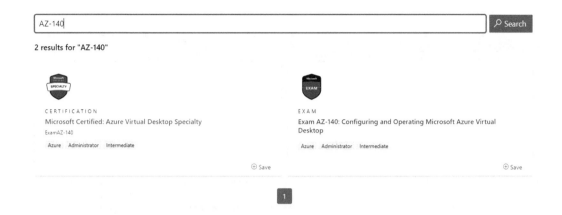

Figure 1-7. *Browsing for the AZ-140 exam*

Figure 1-8 shows the AZ-140 exam page.

Exam AZ-140: Configuring and Operating Microsoft Azure Virtual Desktop

Candidates for this exam are administrators with subject matter expertise in planning, delivering, and managing virtual desktop experiences and remote apps, for any device, on Azure.

Responsibilities for this role include deploying virtual desktop experiences and apps to Azure. Professionals in this role deliver applications on Azure Virtual Desktop and optimize them to run in multi-session virtual environments. To deliver these experiences, they work closely with the Azure administrators and architects, along with Microsoft 365 Administrators.

Candidates for this exam should have experience in Azure technologies, including virtualization, networking, identity, storage, backups, resilience, and disaster recovery. They should understand on-premises virtual desktop infrastructure technologies as they relate to migrating to Azure Virtual Desktop. These professionals use the Azure portal and Azure Resource Manager templates to accomplish many tasks. This role may use PowerShell and Azure Command-Line Interface (CLI) for more efficient automation

Candidates for this exam must have expert Azure administration skills.

Part of the requirements for: Microsoft Certified: Azure Virtual Desktop Specialty
Related exams: none
Important: See details
Go to Certification Dashboard ⬈

Schedule exam

Exam AZ-140: Configuring and Operating Microsoft Azure Virtual Desktop

Languages: English, Japanese, Chinese (Simplified), Korean, French, German, Spanish, Portuguese (Brazil), Russian, Arabic (Saudi Arabia), Chinese (Traditional), Italian
Retirement date: none

This exam measures your ability to accomplish the following technical tasks: plan a Azure Virtual Desktop architecture; implement a Azure Virtual Desktop infrastructure; manage access and security; manage user environments and apps; and monitor and maintain a Azure Virtual Desktop infrastructure.

Figure 1-8. *AZ-140 exam page*

It is recommended that you use this exam page for reference when preparing for the AZ-140 certification. At this stage of the chapter, you should have access to Microsoft Learn to log in and browse for content. The following section explains how to create a trial subscription to the Microsoft 365 services.

Creating a Microsoft 365 and Azure Trial Account

If you are new to Microsoft's cloud services, such as Azure and Microsoft 365, it is important to get hands-on experience, not only for the exam you are taking, but also for professional development. You must understand the Admin Portals and how they work if you are looking to get certified. In this book, we provide exercises that will familiarize you with how to work in the Microsoft 365 and Azure Portals and how to navigate them.

In order to follow along with the steps, we recommend you get a subscription to Microsoft 365. We explain the steps for obtaining a 30-day trial in the next section.

Microsoft 365 Trial Subscription

The features and capabilities discussed in the AZ-140 exam objectives require a Microsoft 365 license. Refer to the "Technical Requirements" section of this chapter for a list of all supported subscriptions. For the purposes of this book, we obtain a Microsoft 365 Business Premium license. Microsoft offers a 30-day trial license, so as you prepare for the exam, you can create these subscriptions and follow the exercises.

You can browse to the following link to get started: `https://www.microsoft.com/en-gb/microsoft-365/business/microsoft-365-business-premium?activetab=pivot%3aoverviewtab`. Select Try Free for 1 Month, as shown in Figure 1-9. Note that you may be prompted to change your country/location when you use this link.

Figure 1-9. *Microsoft 365 Business Premium trial*

You then need to complete the steps outlined in Figure 1-10. You can create a new account or use an existing one.

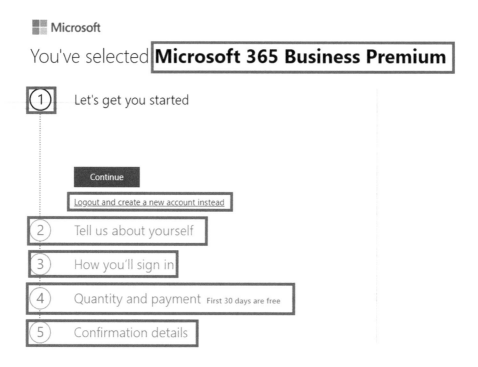

Figure 1-10. *Complete the trial license form*

Once you have completed the process and created the Microsoft 365 tenant, you will have access to the full Microsoft 365 suite of services, as well as all the different admin panels. The next section walks you through the process of setting up an Azure trial service, which is required to follow along with the exercises in this book and complete the hands-on labs.

Obtaining an Azure Subscription

Azure Virtual Desktop is hosted as an Infrastructure as a Service (IaaS) within Microsoft Azure. Therefore, you need to create a trial subscription tenant for Azure to ensure you can follow the lab exercises in this book. You can do this by completing the following steps:

1. Open a web browser and navigate to `https://azure.microsoft.com`.

2. Click Try Azure for Free, as shown in Figure 1-11.

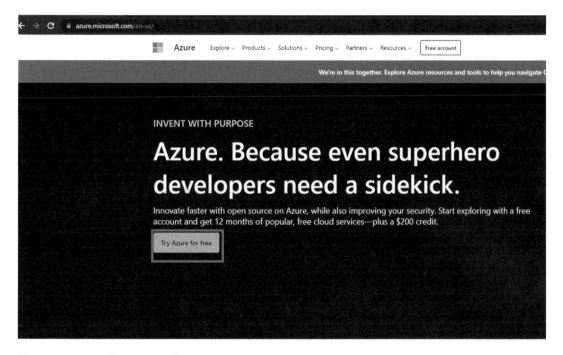

Figure 1-11. *Try Azure for Free*

3. Click Start Free, as shown in Figure 1-12.

Figure 1-12. *Start the Azure trial for free*

4. Log in with an existing Microsoft account or create a new one.

5. Complete the agreement section and the verification process (by phone or credit card), as shown in Figure 1-13, and then click Sign Up.

Figure 1-13. *Complete Azure sign-up*

Introduction to the AZ-140 Exam Objectives

This section covers the exam objectives for the AZ-140 "Configuring and Operating Microsoft Azure Virtual Desktop" exam. The structure of this book closely follows these exam objectives. Each exam objective is weighed differently. The weight of the objective is used as a compass for understanding the knowledge required for that section, as well as a guide to understanding the potential number of questions you can expect on the exam for each specific topic.

The following table lists the objectives covered on the AZ-140 exam:

Objective	Weight
Plan an Azure Virtual Desktop Architecture	10-15%
Implement an Azure Virtual Desktop infrastructure	25-30%
Manage Access and Security	10-15%
Manage User Environments and Apps	20-25%
Monitor & Maintain an Azure Virtual Desktop Infrastructure	20-25%

You can find further details on the topics that are covered on the AZ-140 exam at the following link: `https://query.prod.cms.rt.microsoft.com/cms/api/am/binary/RE4MFST`.

The weight percentage does not mean that an objective with a 10% weight will have 6 questions out of 60. Microsoft exams use a scoring scale of 1000 based on the type of question and objectives covered in that question. The weights of the objectives will aid you in understanding the level of importance placed on the specific objective.

The next section provides information and insight into the types of roles that this exam highlights and explains how the AZ-140 exam can assist you in your professional development.

Why You Should Take This Exam

The AZ-140 exam is the specialist Microsoft Azure Virtual Desktop associate level exam, so the focus is on planning and provisioning the Azure Virtual Desktop platform, as well as other Azure services that integrate with Azure Virtual Desktop. You should take this exam if you have aspirations of working with Azure Virtual Desktop. The exam prepares you for the role of an administrator, specifically in managing Azure Virtual Desktop. It is recommended that you have an associate level understanding of Azure and that you have passed the Azure Administrator certification (AZ-104); however, this is not a requirement.

Introduction to Azure Virtual Desktop

Azure Virtual Desktop, or AVD, is a virtualization service that is cloud-hosted. It allows organizations to virtualize desktop and applications in a secure platform that can be accessed from anywhere and from multiple device types.

AVD enables organizations to offer the following features:

- Create a multi-session Windows 10 desktop that provides a full Windows 10 experience that can easily scale

- Present a Windows 7 virtual desktop that offers extended security updates for free

- Provide Microsoft 365 Apps for enterprises, which can be virtualized and run in a multi-session, multi-user environment

- Allow management of Windows Server, Windows 7, and Windows 10 OS desktops with a cohesive management experience

The next section goes into the key capabilities of Azure Virtual Desktop and their benefits.

Key Capabilities

AVD allows organizations to set up redundant, scalable, and agile environments that offer the following key capabilities:

- Configure an unlimited number of hostpools that can accommodate different workloads in an organization

- Create custom images for your multiple workloads or utilize the ready-to-deploy images in the Azure Gallery for testing

- Integrate Azure services to automate updates, power on/off, and autoscaling to help reduce costs and admin overhead

- Provision personal (persistent) desktops that allow for individual ownership

From a management perspective, you can utilize the Azure Portal, PowerShell, and REST interfaces to manage and implement AVD resources. You can publish a fully featured desktop or a single remote application for different sets of users. You can also assign multiple users to multiple application groups to reduce the number of images.

This section introduced Azure Virtual Desktop and discussed its key capabilities.

Summary

This chapter covered all the areas that will help you prepare for the "Configuring and Operating Azure Virtual Desktop" exam, which includes preparing your account, accessing resources and Microsoft Learn, creating a Microsoft 365 trial account, creating an Azure trial subscription, introducing exam objectives, and a quick overview of why you should take this exam. These key topics give you the understanding and knowledge you need to use Microsoft's free learning resources and create a trial subscription, which will allow you to complete the hands-on labs throughout this book. Additionally, you learned about the types of exam questions you will find on all of Microsoft's role-based exams.

The next chapter looks at how to plan an Azure Virtual Desktop architecture, including designing the architecture for user identities and profiles.

CHAPTER 2

Plan an Azure Virtual Desktop Architecture

The previous chapter introduced the process of getting a Microsoft role-based certification and discussed the steps you need to follow to run the lab exercises throughout this book. The topics that were covered included preparing for a Microsoft exam, accessing resources and Microsoft Learn, creating Microsoft 365 and Azure trial accounts, an introduction to the AZ-140 exam objectives, and an introduction to Azure Virtual Desktop.

This chapter covers the following topics:

- Designing the Azure Virtual Desktop architecture

- Designing the user identities and profiles

Technical Requirements

To complete the exercises in the book, you need to have access to a Microsoft 365 tenant. This can be attained by signing up for a trial subscription. Additionally, Azure Virtual Desktop services require one of the following licenses:

- Microsoft 365 Business Premium

- Microsoft 365 E5/E3

- Microsoft 365 A3/A5/Student Benefits

- Microsoft 365 F3

- Windows 10 Enterprise E3/E5

- Windows 10 Education A3/A5

- Windows 10 VDA per user

© Shabaz Darr 2022
S. Darr, *Azure Virtual Desktop Specialist*, https://doi.org/10.1007/978-1-4842-7987-8_2

Designing the Azure Virtual Desktop Architecture

Azure Virtual Desktop (AVD) is a virtualization service for desktops and applications. This service is hosted in the cloud, but it can integrate with both Azure Cloud and an on-premises infrastructure. This section explores how to design the AVD infrastructure and the components in the service.

Azure Virtual Desktop Architecture

The diagram in Figure 2-1 shows a standard architecture for an AVD environment.

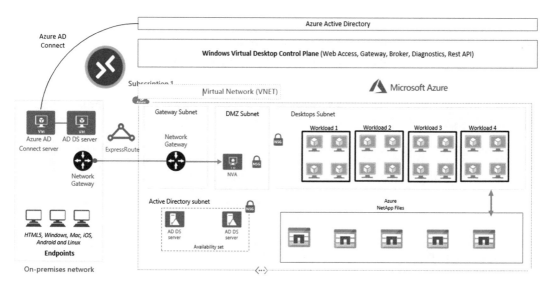

Figure 2-1. *Azure Virtual Desktop typical architecture*

As you can see from the architecture in Figure 2-1, the control panel toward the top takes care of the web access, gateway, broker services, diagnostics, and the components like REST APIs. All the application endpoints are situated in the on-premises infrastructure, which is connected via a site-to-site VPN, or in this case an ExpressRoute. Azure AD connect, which synchronizes the on-premises Active Directory objects with Azure AD, is also situated within the on-premises network.

With this type of Azure Virtual Desktop architecture, it is the customer's responsibility to manage the following services:

- Active Directory domain services

- Azure AD

- Azure subscription

- Virtual networks (VNets)

- Azure files or Azure NetApp file shares

- AVD hostpools and workspaces

This section looked at the Azure Virtual Desktop architecture and some of the services that are part of the platform. The next section takes a closer look at the components that are managed by Microsoft and those that are managed by the end customer.

Components

There are multiple components that combine to make the Azure Virtual Desktop platform; however, not all are managed by a single entity. Some are managed by Microsoft and others by the end customer.

The following components are managed by Microsoft:

- **Web Access:** This component enables the end user to gain access to AVD and the virtual applications via an HTML5-compatible Internet browser. This can be accessed from any device from anywhere as long as there is a secure Internet connection. To increase security you can also utilize multi-factor authentication in Azure AD to control access to this component.

- **Connection broker:** User connections to the remote desktop and remote applications are managed by this component of Azure Virtual Desktop. It delivers load balancing and reconnections to disconnected sessions.

- **Gateway:** This component allows remote users to connect to Azure Virtual Desktop resources from any device that is connected to the Internet. The gateway coordinates a connection from the virtual machine back to the same gateway.

- **Extensibility components:** AVD can be managed by utilizing
  Windows PowerShell or with the REST APIs that are provided, which
  also allows for support from third-party tools.

- **Diagnostics:** This event-based aggregator marks each action (made
  by either a user or administrator) on the AVD deployment as an event
  failure or success. It is then possible to query the event to discover
  any failing components.

The following components are managed by you, the consumer:

- **Azure Active Directory:** AVD uses Azure Active Directory, better
  known as Azure AD, to manage identity and access, better known
  as IAM. We cover this topic in more detail in the "Design for User
  Identities and Profiles" section of this chapter.

- **Azure Virtual Network:** AVD compute resources use the Azure
  Virtual Network, better known as VNet, to communicate privately
  with other Azure compute resources and between the virtual
  machines. You can define network topology to access AVD from the
  Internet or do this internally, based on your organization's policies.
  AVD can also be connected to on-premises infrastructure by utilizing
  a virtual private network (VPN) or an ExpressRoute connection.

- **Active Directory Domain Services (AD DS):** The AVD virtual
  machines must be domain-joined, therefore, there must be a domain
  controller that is accessible in your network. AD DS must have a
  sync with Azure AD, which allows for a single identity to be used to
  access the AVD services. The Azure AD connect service is utilized to
  synchronize on-premises identity objects with Azure AD.

- **AVD Session Hosts:** Session hosts are the virtual machines in a
  hostpool, which can run any of the following operating systems:

  - Windows Server 2012 R2 and above

  - Windows 7 Enterprise

  - Windows 10 Enterprise

  - Windows 10 Enterprise multi-session

  - Custom image with preloaded configuration

You can customize the VM size, which includes the amount of
virtual CPU, better known as vCPU, memory (RAM), and GPU-
enabled virtual machines. Every session host will have an AVD
host agent installed by default, which will register the session host
into the workspace/tenant.

- **AVD Workspace:** Also known as the AVD tenant, this is the service
  that manages the session hosts and publishes the hostpool resources.

This section reviewed the components of Azure Virtual Desktop that are managed by
Microsoft and the components that are managed by the consumer. In the next section,
we look at personal and pooled desktops.

Pooled and Personal Desktops

Pooled desktops are also referred to as non-persistent desktops, whereby users are
assigned to the application group of the desktop and connect to any available session host.
The session host the user connects to is based on one of two load-balancing algorithms.
The first is *breadth-first,* whereby the algorithm is utilized to determine the smallest
number of sessions on a session host and then new connections are placed on that host.

 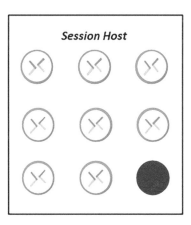

Figure 2-2. *Breadth-first load balancing placement diagram*

Figure 2-2 shows the breadth-fist method of load balancing, which is based on
the least number of sessions on a host. The session host on the left side has more
connections, so the session host on the right side will take the next connection that is
made, indicated by the red circle.

The other algorithm is the *depth-first* load balancing method. It's based on session host utilization. This method connects users to a single session host and maximizes its compute resources before it loads connections and sessions on the next available session host. This algorithm is better suited to businesses and organizations that want to run an active/passive AVD solution, or to reduce costs.

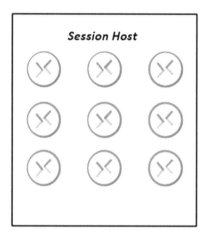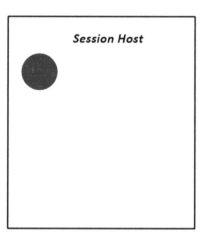

Figure 2-3. *Depth-first Load balancing algorithm*

Figure 2-3 shows that the session host on the left side has a maximum number of connections, so the next available session connection will be made to the session host on the right side, signified by the red circle.

In this section, we discussed the two session host load-balancing methods and how they operate. The next section discusses setting up Azure resources and assigning roles and licenses.

Setting Up Azure Resources and Assigning Roles and Licenses

Before you start to provision any AVD-specific services, you need to create and configure the underlying Azure services. As part of your preparation, you need to create the following resources in Azure:

- **Resource Group:** You can create multiple resource groups or a single resource group to host your Azure resources.

The following steps explain how to create an Azure Resource Group from the Azure Portal:

1. Log in to your Microsoft Azure trial account you set up in Chapter 1. On the Azure Portal home page, navigate to the search bar at the top of the screen and type **Resource Groups**. Then select it from the results, as shown in Figure 2-4.

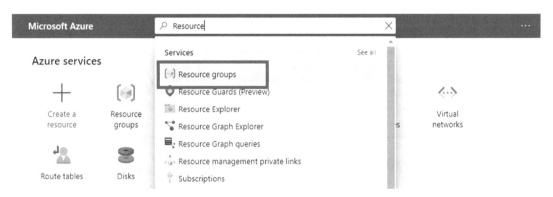

Figure 2-4. *Search for the Azure Resource Groups*

2. In the Resource Groups pane, click Create, as shown in Figure 2-5.

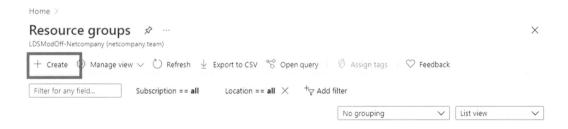

Figure 2-5. *Create a Resource Group*

3. On the Create a Resource Group page, enter the relevant details (see Figure 2-6):

   - **Subscription:** Select the relevant subscription. In this case, this will be the trial subscription you set up in Chapter 1.

   - **Resource Group**: Enter an appropriate name you want to give your resource group.

- **Region:** Specify a region where you want your resources to reside. This should normally be local to the country where you live, but it is possible to utilize a resource group in a different region.

4. Click Next.

Home > Resource groups >

Create a resource group ...

Basics   Tags   Review + create

Resource group - A container that holds related resources for an Azure solution. The resource group can include all the resources for the solution, or only those resources that you want to manage as a group. You decide how you want to allocate resources to resource groups based on what makes the most sense for your organization. Learn more ⌕

Project details

Subscription * ⓘ   ⌄

Resource group * ⓘ   AZ-140RG   ✓

Resource details

Region * ⓘ   (Europe) UK South   ⌄

Review + create   < Previous   Next : Tags >

Figure 2-6. *Basic resource group information*

5. On the Tags window, you can enter a name and value to tag
    your resource group. An example of this is giving a name of
    Department and a value of Marketing. In this example, we leave
    this blank and click Next to move on.

6. On the Review + Create page, review the settings and ensure the
    validation passes. If it does not, you need to review the error and
    fix it before moving on. Click Create, as shown in Figure 2-7.

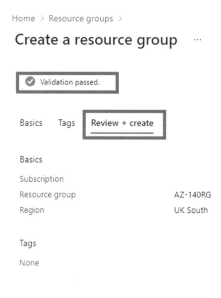

Figure 2-7. *Validation page*

The following lab exercise explains how to create a resource group from PowerShell:

1. You first need to install the Azure AZ PowerShell module. Follow the steps in the following link to install it on the computer you are completing the lab exercises on: `https://docs.microsoft.com/en-us/powershell/azure/install-az-ps?view=azps-6.6.0`.

2. Once the installation is completed, launch PowerShell with administrator privileges. Use the command shown in Figure 2-8 to sign in.

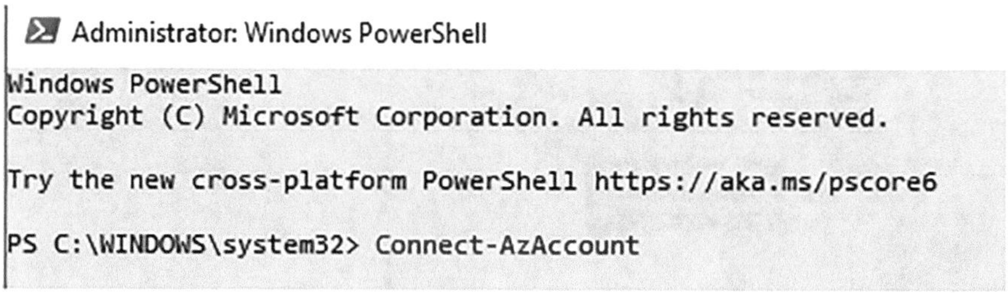

```
 Administrator: Windows PowerShell
Windows PowerShell
Copyright (C) Microsoft Corporation. All rights reserved.

Try the new cross-platform PowerShell https://aka.ms/pscore6

PS C:\WINDOWS\system32> Connect-AzAccount
```

Figure 2-8. *Connect to Azure PowerShell*

3. This will launch a Microsoft username and password prompt. Enter your Global Administrator credentials, as shown in Figure 2-9.

Sign in to your account   ✕

Microsoft Azure

■■ Microsoft

Sign in

Email address, phone number or Skype

No account? Create one!

Can't access your account?

Back   Next

🔑   Sign-in options

Figure 2-9. *Microsoft credentials window*

4. When the authentication is complete, you will see the screen
    shown in Figure 2-10 in PowerShell.

```
PS C:\WINDOWS\system32> Connect-AzAccount

Account                 SubscriptionName         TenantId              Environment
-------                 ----------------         --------              -----------
shabaz.admin@r                                                         AzureCloud


PS C:\WINDOWS\system32>
```

Figure 2-10. *Azure PowerShell login completed*

5. Enter the command shown in Figure 2-11 to create an Azure
    Resource Group.

```
PS C:\WINDOWS\system32> New-AzResourceGroup -Name AVDRG01 -Location "uksouth"
```

Figure 2-11. *Create an Azure Resource Group via PowerShell*

- **Virtual network:** This is required in order to provision a hostpool.
  The VNet needs to be connected to the AD DS domain and must
  enable outbound access to the URLs listed in Table 2-1.

Table 2-1. *Required URL Access*

Address	Outbound TCP Port	Objective	Service Tag
*.wvd.microsoft.com	443	Service Traffic	WindowsVirtualDesktop
mrsglobalsteus2prod.blob. core.windows.net	443	Agent and SXS stack updates	AzureCloud
*.core.windows.net	443	Agent Traffic	AzueCloud
*.servicebus.windows.net	443	Agent Traffic	AzureCloud
Prod.warmpath. msftcloudes.com	443	Agent Traffic	AzureCloud
catalogartifact. azureedge.net	443	Azure Marketplace	AzureCloud
kms.core.windows.net	1688	Windows activation	Internet
wvdportalstorageblob. blob.core.windows.net	443	Azure Portal support	AzureCloud

The following steps explain how to create an Azure Virtual Network (VNet):

1. On the Azure Portal home page, navigate to the search bar at the
    top of the screen and type **virtual networks**. Select the service to
    navigate to the Virtual Networks menu, as shown in Figure 2-12.

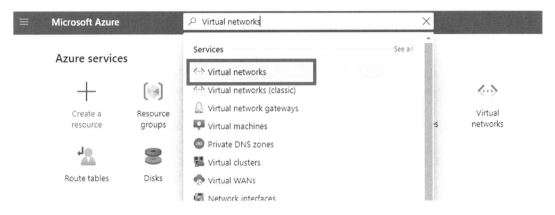

Figure 2-12. *Navigate to the Virtual Networks menu*

2. Click + Create to navigate to the Create Virtual Network window, as shown in Figure 2-13.

Figure 2-13. *Create a Virtual Network*

3. On the Basics pane, enter the relevant details as follows:

    •   **Subscription:** Select the relevant subscription. In this case, this will be the trial subscription you set up in Chapter 1.

    •   **Resource Group**: Select the resource group that was created in the lab earlier in this chapter.

    •   **Name:** Enter the name you want to give your virtual network.

    •   ***Region:*** Specify a region where you want your resources to reside. This should normally be local to the country where you live. Click Next, as shown in Figure 2-14.

Home > Virtual networks >

Create virtual network   ⋯

| **Basics** | IP Addresses | Security | Tags | Review + create |

Azure Virtual Network (VNet) is the fundamental building block for your private network in Azure. VNet enables many types of Azure resources, such as Azure Virtual Machines (VM), to securely communicate with each other, the internet, and on-premises networks. VNet is similar to a traditional network that you'd operate in your own data center, but brings with it additional benefits of Azure's infrastructure such as scale, availability, and isolation. Learn more about virtual network

Project details

Subscription * ⓘ

Resource group * ⓘ	AZ-140RG	⌄
	Create new	

Instance details

Name *	AZ-140-vNET	✓

Region *	(Europe) UK South	⌄

Figure 2-14. *Virtual network basic information*

4. On the IP Addresses window, type an IPV4 address space that meets your requirements. ***Note:*** You need to ensure the IP range you select does not clash with any existing virtual networks, on-premises networks you want to integrate with, or any existing Azure networks in different regions you want to peer with in the future.

5. You can then either leave the default subnet in place or create a new subnet and delete the default one. For the purposes of this lab exercise, we use the default subnet and click Next, as shown in Figure 2-15.

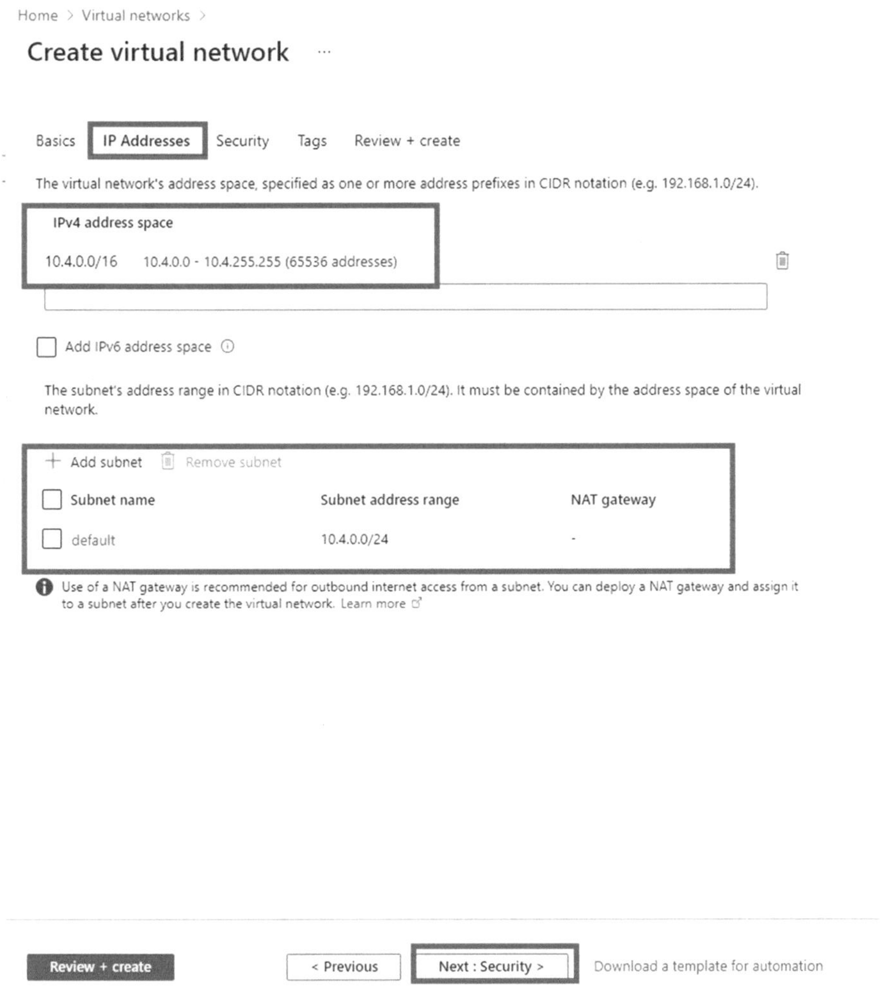

Figure 2-15. *Configure IP address space*

6. On the Security tab, you can enable the following services:

    • **BastionHost**: This service is a new, fully platform-managed PaaS
      service that you provision inside your virtual network. It provides
      a secure and seamless RDP/SSH connectivity to your virtual
      machines directly in the Azure Portal over SSL.

- **Distributed Denial-of-Service (DDoS) Protection Standard**: The standard DDoS protection plan is a paid service that offers enhanced DDoS mitigation capabilities via adaptive tuning, attack notification, and telemetry to protect against the impacts of a DDoS attack for all resources connected to your virtual network.

- **Firewall**: Azure Firewall is a managed, cloud-based network security service that protects your virtual network resource.

For the purposes of this lab exercise, we leave all these services disabled and click Next. See Figure 2-16.

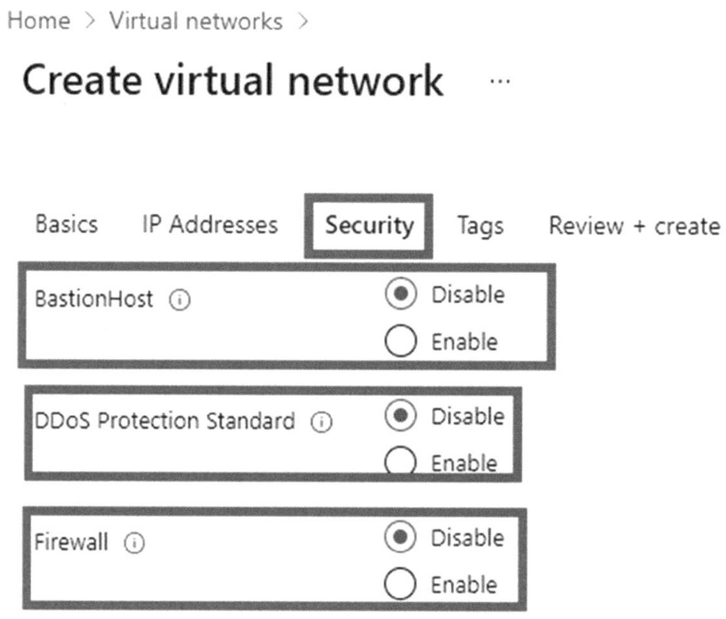

Figure 2-16. *Security section*

7. On the Tags tab, you can enter a name and value to tag your resource group. An example of this is giving a name of Department and a value of Marketing. In this example, we leave this blank and click Next to move on.

8. On the Review + Create page, review the settings and ensure the validation passes. If it does not pass, you need to review the error and fix it before moving on. Click Create. At this point, the deployment page will show the steps being completed. See Figure 2-17.

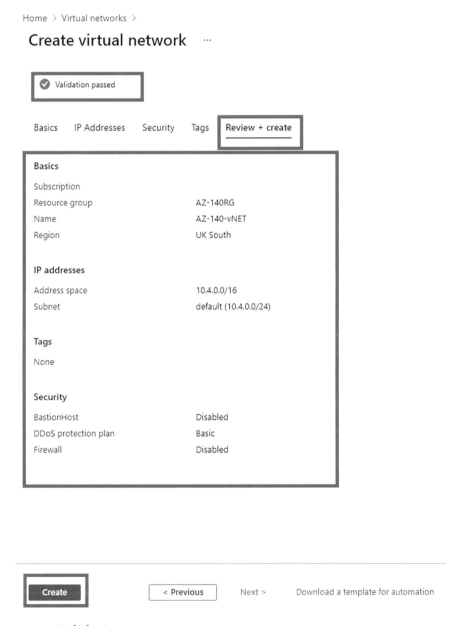

Figure 2-17. *Validation page*

The following lab exercise explains how to create a virtual network in Azure using PowerShell:

1. Install PowerShell and use the instruction from earlier in the chapter to log in to Azure via PowerShell.

2. Use the command shown in Figure 2-18 to create a virtual network. This example uses the following settings:

    - Name = AVDVNET

    - Resource Group = AVDRG

    - Location = UK South

    - IP Address Prefix = 10.9.0.0/16

```
PS C:\WINDOWS\system32> $vnet = @{
>>      Name = 'AVDVNET'
>>      ResourceGroupName = 'AVDRG01'
>>      Location = 'UkSouth'
>>      AddressPrefix = '10.9.0.0/16'
>> }
PS C:\WINDOWS\system32> $virtualNetwork = New-AzVirtualNetwork @vnet
```

Figure 2-18. *Create a virtual network with PowerShell*

3. Use the command shown in Figure 2-19 to add a subnet to the network. This example uses the following subnet settings:

    - Name = Default

    - Virtual network = using $virtualnetwork for the AVDVNET

    - Address prefix = 10.9.0.0/24

```
PS C:\WINDOWS\system32> $subnet = @{
>>      Name = 'default'
>>      VirtualNetwork = $virtualNetwork
>>      AddressPrefix = '10.9.0.0/24'
>> }
PS C:\WINDOWS\system32> $subnetConfig = Add-AzVirtualNetworkSubnetConfig @subnet
```

Figure 2-19. *Add a subnet to the virtual network*

- **Storage Account:** This service is utilized to store virtual disk files that are used with FSLogix and to create Azure File share services for AVD session hosts. You have the choice of using Azure NetApp files or Storage Spaces Direct. For more information on Azure NetApp files, visit `https://docs.microsoft.com/en-us/azure/azure-netapp-files/azure-netapp-files-introduction`. For more information on Storage Spaces Direct, visit `https://docs.microsoft.com/en-us/windows-server/storage/storage-spaces/storage-spaces-direct-overview`.

The following lab exercise explains how to create a storage account via the Azure Portal:

1. On the Azure Portal home page, navigate to the search bar at the top of the screen and type **storage accounts**. Select the service to navigate to the Storage Accounts menu, as shown in Figure 2-20.

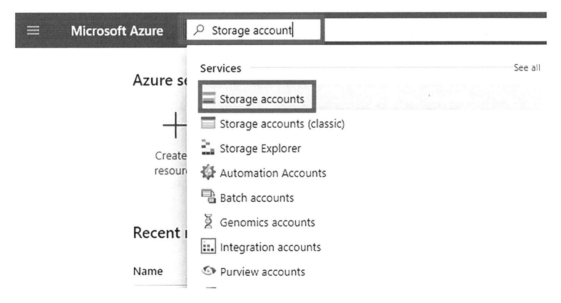

Figure 2-20. *Navigate to Storage Accounts service*

2. From the Storage Account menu, click + Create to start the
    configuration wizard, as shown in Figure 2-21.

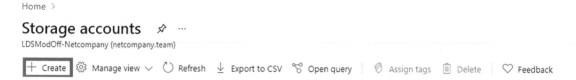

Figure 2-21. *Create a storage account*

3. On the Create Storage Account page, enter the relevant details as
    follows:

    - **Subscription:** Select the relevant subscription. In this case, this
      will be the trial subscription you set up in Chapter 1.

    - **Resource Group**: Select the resource group that was created in
      the lab earlier in this chapter.

    - **Name:** Enter the name you want to give your storage account.
      Note that this name needs to be in lowercase and unique within
      Azure globally, not just in your own tenant.

    - **Region:** Specify a region where you want your resources to reside.
      This should normally be local to the country where you live.

    - **Performance:** You have two choices here: Standard or Premium.
      We will need to provision Azure files in future chapters, so we
      need to provision a Premium storage account.

    - **Premium Account Type:** From the drop-down, select
      File Shares.

    - *Redundancy*: Select the relevant redundancy type that matches
      your requirements. For the purposes of this exercise, we select
      Locally-Redundant Storage (LRS). Click Next. See Figure 2-22.

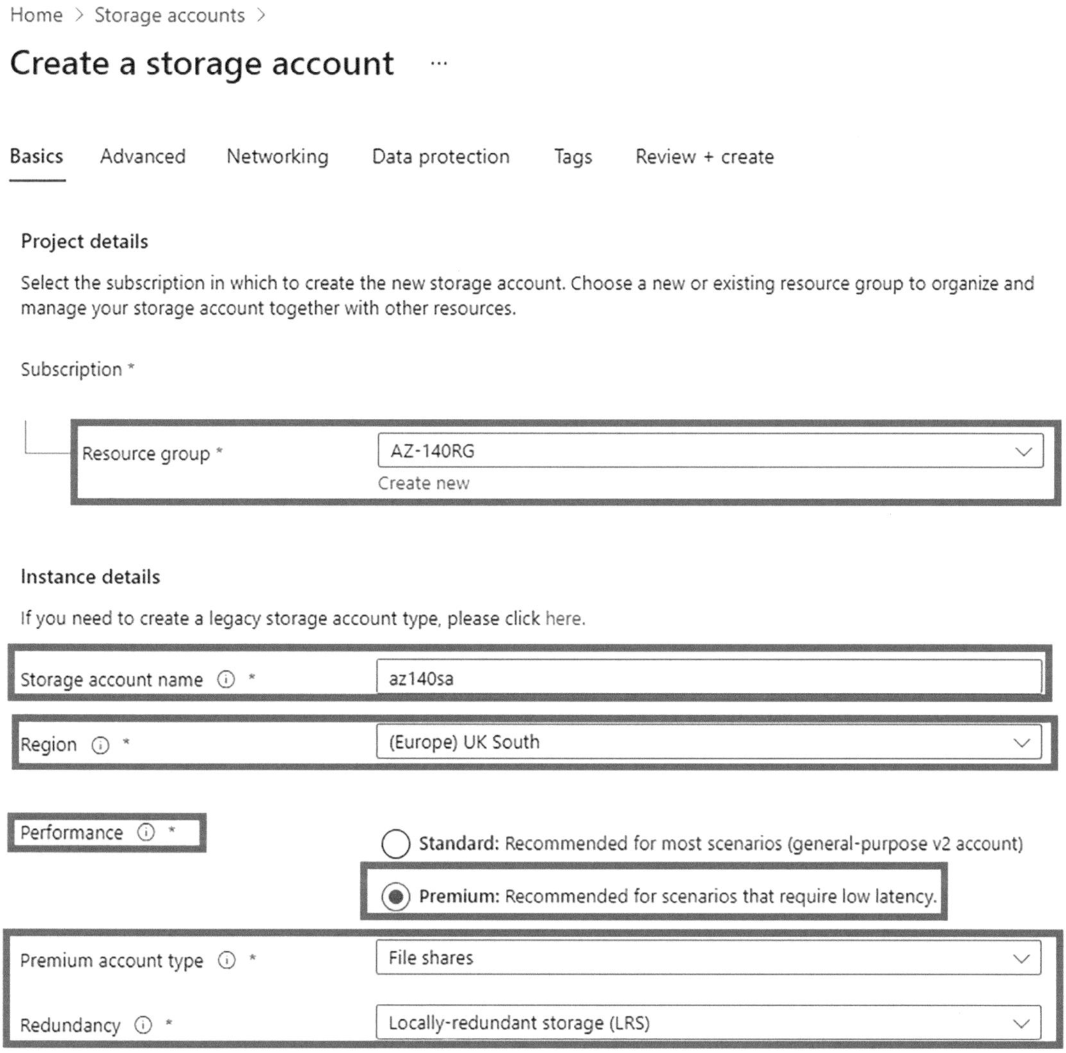

Home > Storage accounts >

Create a storage account   ⋯

Basics   Advanced   Networking   Data protection   Tags   Review + create

Project details

Select the subscription in which to create the new storage account. Choose a new or existing resource group to organize and manage your storage account together with other resources.

Subscription *

Resource group *   AZ-140RG   ∨
                                    Create new

Instance details

If you need to create a legacy storage account type, please click here.

Storage account name ⓘ *   az140sa

Region ⓘ *   (Europe) UK South   ∨

Performance ⓘ *   ○ **Standard:** Recommended for most scenarios (general-purpose v2 account)

                                   ⦿ **Premium:** Recommended for scenarios that require low latency.

Premium account type ⓘ *   File shares   ∨

Redundancy ⓘ *   Locally-redundant storage (LRS)   ∨

Figure 2-22. *Complete Basic information tab*

4. On the Advanced tab, you can configure the following settings:

    • Security

    • Data Lake Storage Gen2

    • Blob Storage

    • Azure Files

    • Tables and Queues

For the purpose of this lab exercise, we leave all these settings as
the defaults and click Next. See Figure 2-23.

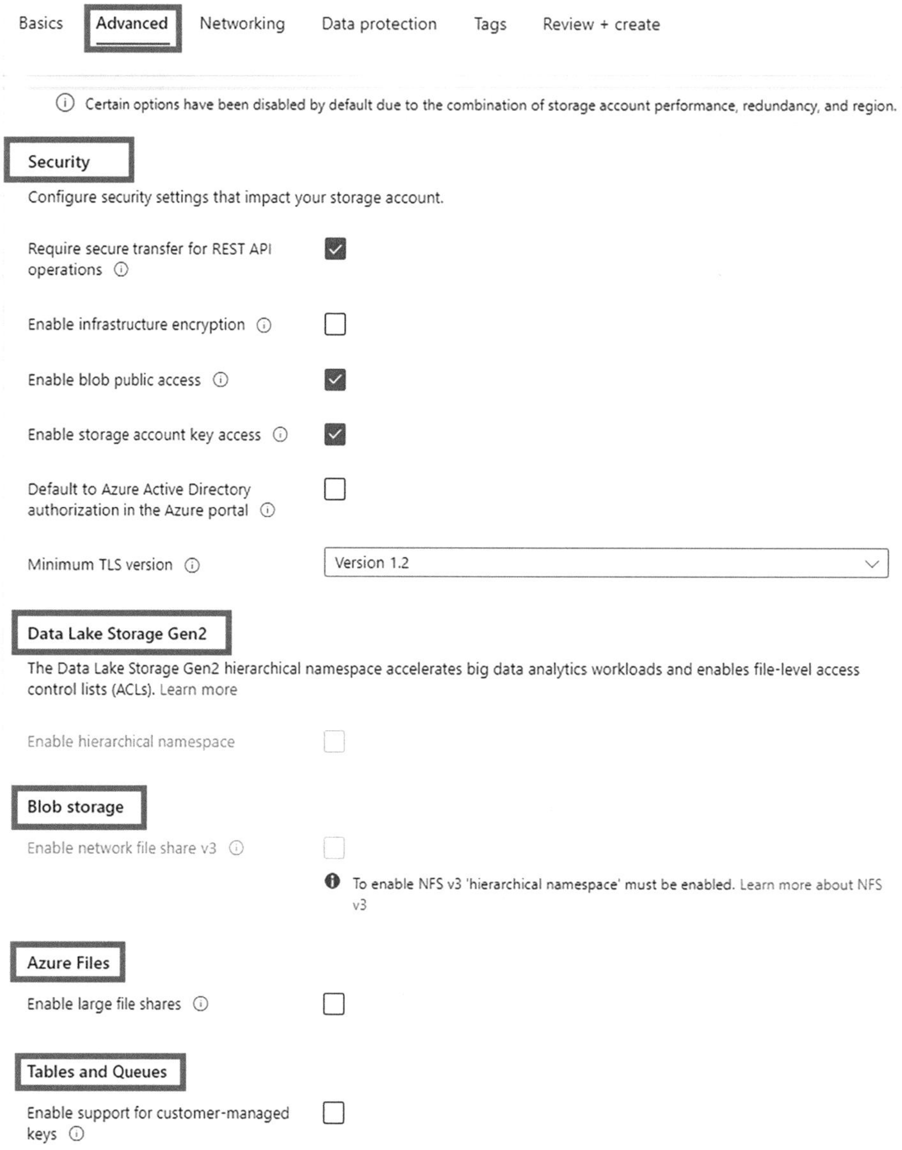

Figure 2-23. *Storage Account advanced settings*

5. On the Networking tab, you have the option to configure Network
    Connectivity and Network Routing.

- **Connectivity method:** For this setting, you can choose Public Endpoint (All Networks) if you can leave it open to everyone, Public Endpoint (Selected Networks) if you want to leave it open to only specific subnets, or Private Endpoint if you want to configure a private endpoint for high security.

- **Network routing:** You have the option of choosing Microsoft Routing or Internet Routing.

For the purposes of this lab exercise, we leave all the settings on the defaults. Click Next. See Figure 2-24.

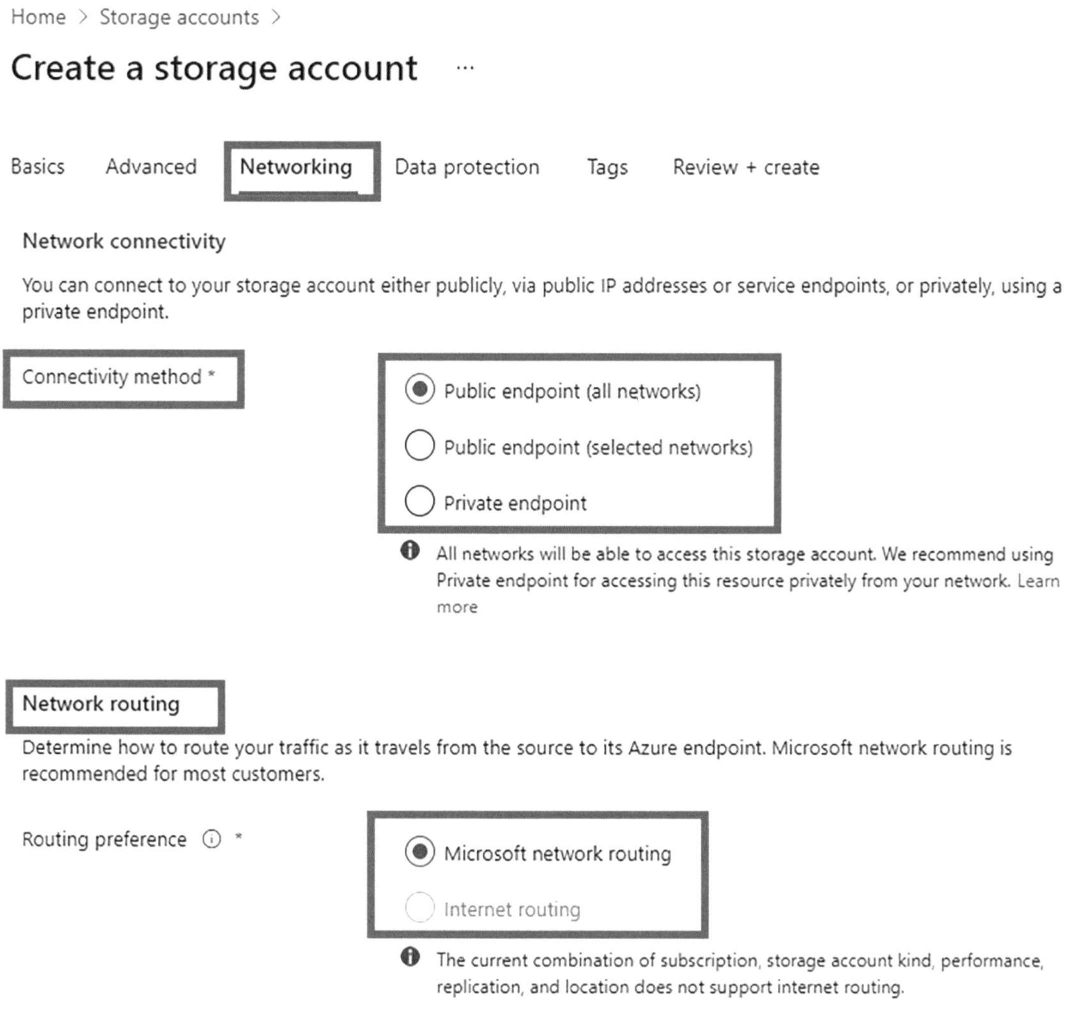

Home > Storage accounts >

Create a storage account ...

Basics   Advanced | Networking | Data protection   Tags   Review + create

Network connectivity

You can connect to your storage account either publicly, via public IP addresses or service endpoints, or privately, using a private endpoint.

Connectivity method *

- ● Public endpoint (all networks)
- ○ Public endpoint (selected networks)
- ○ Private endpoint

ⓘ All networks will be able to access this storage account. We recommend using Private endpoint for accessing this resource privately from your network. Learn more

Network routing

Determine how to route your traffic as it travels from the source to its Azure endpoint. Microsoft network routing is recommended for most customers.

Routing preference ⓘ *

- ● Microsoft network routing
- ○ Internet routing

ⓘ The current combination of subscription, storage account kind, performance, replication, and location does not support internet routing.

Figure 2-24. *Storage account networking*

6. On the Data Protection tab, you have the option of configuring Recovery and Tracking. For the purposes of this lab exercise, we leave all default settings in place. Click Next. See Figure 2-25.

| Basics | Advanced | Networking | **Data protection** | Tags | Review + create |

ⓘ Certain options have been disabled by default due to the combination of storage account performance, redundancy, and region.

Recovery

Protect your data from accidental or erroneous deletion or modification.

☐ Enable point-in-time restore for containers

Use point-in-time restore to restore one or more containers to an earlier state. If point-in-time restore is enabled, then versioning, change feed, and blob soft delete must also be enabled. Learn more

☐ Enable soft delete for blobs

Soft delete enables you to recover blobs that were previously marked for deletion, including blobs that were overwritten. Learn more

☐ Enable soft delete for containers

Soft delete enables you to recover containers that were previously marked for deletion. Learn more

☑ Enable soft delete for file shares

Soft delete enables you to recover file shares that were previously marked for deletion. Learn more

Days to retain deleted file shares ⓘ   7

Tracking

Manage versions and keep track of changes made to your blob data.

☐ Enable versioning for blobs

Use versioning to automatically maintain previous versions of your blobs for recovery and restoration. Learn more

☐ Enable blob change feed

Keep track of create, modification, and delete changes to blobs in your account. Learn more

Figure 2-25. *Storage Account Data Protection settings*

7. On the Tags tab, you can enter a name and value for your resource group. An example of this is giving a name of Department and a value of Marketing. In this example, we will leave this blank and click Next to move on.

8. On the Review + Create page, review the settings and ensure the validation passes. If it does not pass, you need to review the error and fix it before moving on. Click Create.

The following lab exercise explains how to create a storage account with PowerShell:

1. Install PowerShell and use the instructions from earlier in the chapter to log in to Azure via PowerShell.

2. Use the command shown in Figure 2-26 to create a Premium Storage account. This example has the following settings:

   - Resource Group: ITGEEKRG01

   - Location: UKSouth

   - Storage Account name: itgeeksa02

   - **SkuName**: Premium_LRS

   - Storage type: FileStorage

```
PS C:\WINDOWS\system32> $resourceGroup = "ITGEEKRG01"
PS C:\WINDOWS\system32> $location = "UkSouth"
PS C:\WINDOWS\system32> New-AzStorageAccount -ResourceGroupName $resourceGroup `
>>    -Name itgeeksa02 `
>>    -Location $location `
>>    -SkuName Premium_LRS `
>>    -Kind FileStorage
```

Figure 2-26. *Create a storage account in PowerShell*

   - **Azure Accounts:** It is a best practice recommendation to assign administrator roles to different users in your organization and to create multiple users in each role.

This section covered creating various Azure resources, including resource groups, virtual networks, and storage accounts, via the Azure Portal and PowerShell. In the next section of this chapter, we dive into user identities and profiles.

Designing for User Identities and Profiles

Azure Virtual Desktop does not support external profile or identities at the time of writing this book. Therefore, you must create an Active Directory Domain and associate it with an Azure Active Directory tenant.

Identity Requirements

When designing and configuring Azure Virtual Desktop user identities, you need to meet some specific requirements and follow these guidelines:

- Identities must have an object in both Active Directory and Azure Active Directory. These are also known as hybrid identities. Active Directory Domain Services (AD DS) on-premises or Azure Active Directory Domain Services (AAD DS) create and sync these identities with Azure AD.

- If you are deploying Azure Virtual Desktop to multiple organizations, it is a best practice recommendation deploy a different Azure ad tenant for each organization, as this will mitigate the risk of security breaches.

Before you follow any of the lab exercises in this book, you need to ensure you have set up your Microsoft 365 subscription and your Azure Tenant trial subscription as explained in Chapter 1.

Configuring a Consistent Sign-In Experience

Managing different user accounts and passwords for multiple platforms and systems can make life difficult for users. This can also cause security risks, as users are more likely to use the same password for various platforms.

Microsoft recommends utilizing Azure to create a consistent sign-in experience to ensure users can have the same username, password and security controls for both Microsoft Cloud and on-premises environments. This can be achieved by synchronizing identity objects from on-premises Active Directory Domain Services to Azure AD.

There are multiple options you can utilize to sync identity objects, which can all be set up by configuring Azure AD Connect:

- *Password hash-sync:* In this option, usernames and password hashes are synchronized from AD DS and Azure AD.

- *Passthrough authentication:* This option requires minimal on-premises configuration and enables the AD DS services to accomplish a simple authentication via the cloud services.

- Active Directory Federation Services (ADFS): This option requires more on-premises configuration and is the most complex. Allows you to utilize RSA tokens, complex partner federation, and smartcard authentication.

Active Directory Domain Services for AVD

AD DS is used by Azure Virtual Desktop in the same way that existing virtual desktop infrastructures (VDI) use it for session logins. The following options are available to allow organizations to connect with or configure AD DS with AVD:

- *Configure a Windows Server in Azure and configure the Domain Controller role:* The virtual machine is connected to a virtual network, and it has the Windows Domain Controller role configured on it. This option is the least expensive, but you must manage the virtual machine and ensure it stays fully patched, highly available, and accessible from the network that hosts your AVD session hosts. See Figure 2-27.

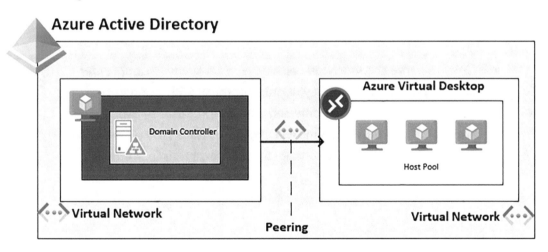

Figure 2-27.   Active Directory Domain Services VM in Azure integration with AVD

- *Configure Azure Active Directory Domain Services (AAD DS):* This
  option is similar to the first one, but it's a Domain Controller as a
  Service, so you do not have to manage a virtual machine, worry about
  patching, or high availability. You can connect the AAD DS tenant to
  the same network as the one that hosts your AVD session hosts. See
  Figure 2-28.

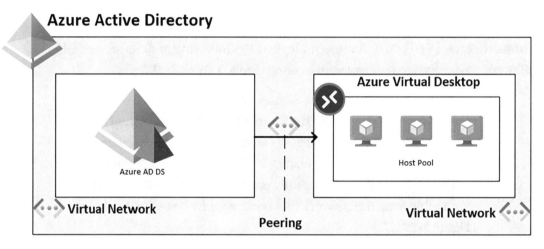

Figure 2-28. *Azure Active Directory Domain Services integration with AVD*

- *Create a network connection between your on-premises/datacenter
  and Azure:* In this scenario, you must establish a VPN or Azure
  ExpressRoute connection between your on-premises network
  and your Azure network. This will allow the Azure Virtual Desktop
  Session Hosts to securely connect to your on-premises Domain
  Controllers. See Figure 2-29.

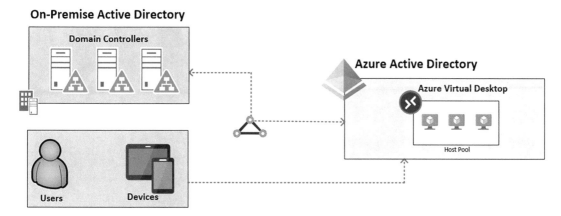

Figure 2-29. *On-Premises Domain Controller integration with Azure Virtual Desktop*

This section looked at the different identity synchronization options as well as the different options you can utilize to configure the Active Directory Domain Services for AVD. The next section looks at assigning licenses to users from the Microsoft 365 Portal and PowerShell and registering the AVD provider with your subscription.

Assigning Microsoft 365 Licenses

Users need to have a Microsoft 365 license assigned to their Azure AD user object before they can access any Azure Virtual Desktop resources. The full list of applicable licenses is discussed earlier, in the "Technical Requirements" section of this chapter. There are two methods for assigning licenses—from the Active Users page or from the Licenses page.

Assign Microsoft 365 Licenses via the Licenses Page in the Admin Portal

The following steps cover assigning licenses from the Licenses page:

1. Log in to the Microsoft 365 Admin Portal via the `https://portal. office.com` link with a Global Admin account. Navigate to the Admin Center.

2. In the Admin Center, navigate to the Billing ➤ Licenses page, as shown in Figure 2-30.

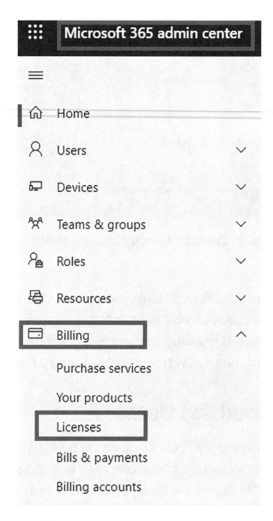

Figure 2-30. *Navigate to the Licenses page*

3. Choose the product you want to assign a license for. In this
    example, we use Microsoft 365 E5 licenses. See Figure 2-31.

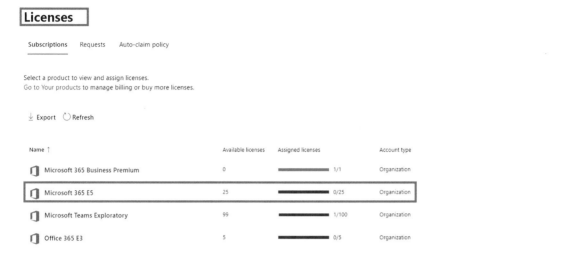

Figure 2-31. *Select the relevant license you want to assign*

4. Click Assign Licenses and then enter the user's email address that
    you want to assign the licenses to. See Figure 2-32.

Figure 2-32. *Assign licenses to users email address*

5. Click Assign.

Assign Microsoft 365 Licenses via the Active Users Page in the Admin Portal

The following steps cover how to assign licenses via the Active Users page.

1. In the Admin Center, navigate to Users ➤ Active Users, as shown in Figure 2-33.

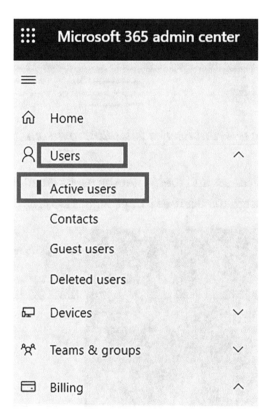

Figure 2-33. *Navigate to the Active Users page*

2. Select the user that you would like to assign the license to, as shown in Figure 2-34.

Figure 2-34. *Select the relevant user to assign the license to*

3. From the user's properties pane on the right side, click License and Apps and select the relevant license, as shown in Figure 2-35. Click Save.

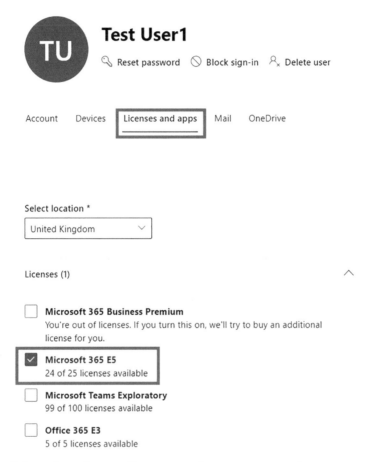

Figure 2-35. *Select the relevant license on the user properties page*

Now we you have added licenses to the user's Azure AD identity from the Admin Center, we will look at assigning licenses via PowerShell.

1. First, you need to ensure you have the Microsoft Azure Active Directory Module for Windows PowerShell installed, and then connect to Azure with the relevant Global Admin credentials. Follow the steps in this link to complete these steps: `https://docs.microsoft.com/en-us/microsoft-365/enterprise/connect-to-microsoft-365-powershell?view=o365-worldwide#connect-with-the-microsoft-azure-active-directory-module-for-windows-powershell`.

2. You can only assign licenses to user accounts that have a
    UsageLocation set. Run the cmdlet shown in Figure 2-36 to find
    users who do not have a UsageLocation value.

```
PS C:\WINDOWS\system32> Get-MsolUser -All | where {$_.UsageLocation -eq $null}
```

Figure 2-36. *Find user accounts without the UsageLocation setting configured*

3. The cmdlet shown in Figure 2-37 will set the UsageLocation value.

```
PS C:\WINDOWS\system32> Set-MsolUser -UserPrincipalName "Test.User1@          -UsageLocation UK
```

Figure 2-37. *Set the UsageLocation for a user account*

4. To assign a license to a user, you need to obtain the AccountSkuId.
    The part before the colon (:) is the domain name. You can get this
    information be running the cmdlet shown in Figure 2-38.

```
PS C:\WINDOWS\system32> Get-MsolAccountSku

AccountSkuId                  ActiveUnits WarningUnits ConsumedUnits
------------                  ----------- ------------ -------------
        :VISIOCLIENT          0           0            0
        :ENTERPRISEPACK       5           0            0
        :SPB                  1           0            1
        :TEAMS_EXPLORATORY    100         0            1
        :SPE_E5               25          0            1
```

Figure 2-38. *Find the relevant license SKU*

5. To assign a license, use the cmdlet shown in Figure 2-39. In this
    example, we assign a license to Test.User1@domain.com and use
    the SPE_E5 SKU.

```
PS C:\WINDOWS\system32> Set-MsolUserLicense -UserPrincipalName "Test.User1          -AddLicenses "IamITGeek:SPE_E5"
```

Figure 2-39. *Assign a license to a user*

In this section, we completed the lab exercises to assign a license to a user from
the Microsoft 365 Admin Center and via PowerShell. The next section looks at how to
register an AVD provider with the subscription.

Microsoft.DesktopVirtualzation Provider Registration

This configuration is the final step in preparing your deployment. You need to authorize the AVD service provider in your subscription.

1. Sign in to the Azure Portal with a Global Admin account by using the following link: `https://portal.azure.com`.

2. Navigate to the Subscriptions page by utilizing the search box at the top of the screen.

3. Click the relevant subscription where you want to register the Azure Virtual Desktop service provider.

4. Navigate to Settings ➤ Resource Providers, as shown in Figure 2-40.

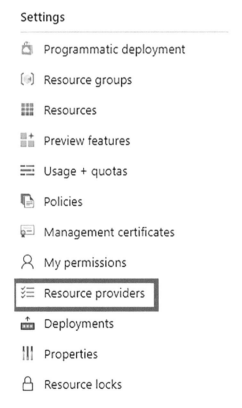

Figure 2-40. *Access the Resource Providers settings*

5. Using the filter box at the top of the window, type **Microsoft.
DestopVirtualization** and then select it in the middle pane, as
shown in Figure 2-41. Click Register.

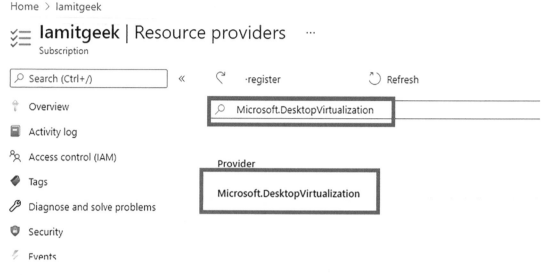

Figure 2-41.

Once this is completed, you will see the status change to Registered. In this section,
you completed the resource provider registration for the Azure Virtual Desktop to the
subscription. The next section tests what you have learned in this chapter so far with
several knowledge check questions.

Knowledge Check

The following questions are aimed at testing your understanding of the information in
this chapter. It is best to complete all sections and labs in this chapter before attempting
these questions.

Check Your Knowledge

1. Which components of Azure Virtual Desktop are managed by
Microsoft? (Select the three best answers.)

   • Web Access

   • Azure AD

- Gateway

- Diagnostics

- Virtual networks

2. Which components of Azure Virtual Desktop are managed by the end user? (Select the three best answers.)

- Connection Broker

- Extensibility components

- AVD Workspace

- Session Hosts

- Active Directory Domain Servers

3. True or False: Pooled hostpools are referred to as non-persistent desktops?

- True

- False

4. What type of storage account do you need to provision with Azure Virtual Desktop to be able to create Azure File shares?

- Standard General-Purpose v2

- Premium Block Blobs

- Premium File Shares

- Premium Page Blobs

5. Which identity sync type synchronizes usernames and password hashes?

- Passthrough authentication

- Password hash-sync

- Active Directory

6. Which resource provider do you need to register with your Azure
    subscription before provisioning Azure Virtual Desktop?

    - Microsoft.Devices

    - Microsoft.VirtualMachineImages

    - Microsoft.DesktopVirtualization

    - Microsoft.DeploymentManager

Summary

This chapter looked at the Azure Virtual Desktop design, components within
the platform, pooled and personal hostpools, and the different types of identity
management. You also completed several lab exercises, including provisioning the
underlying infrastructure (resource groups, virtual networks, and storage accounts) via
the Azure Admin Portal and PowerShell, assigning the relevant Microsoft 365 license to
users via the Microsoft 365 Admin Portal and PowerShell, and registering the resource
provider with your subscription.

Chapter 3 takes a deep dive into implementing Azure Virtual Desktop infrastructure,
including implementing and managing networking for Azure Virtual Desktop,
implementing and managing storage for Azure Virtual Desktop, creating and configuring
hostpools and session hosts, and creating and managing session host images.

CHAPTER 3

Implement an Azure Virtual Desktop Infrastructure

The previous chapter took a deep look into planning the Azure Virtual Desktop Architecture, including the various components that are managed by Microsoft and by the end user, deploying the underlying infrastructure via the admin center and PowerShell, and registering the resource provider with the subscription.

This chapter covers the following main topics:

- Implementing and managing networking for Azure Virtual Desktop

- Implementing and managing storage for Azure Virtual Desktop

- Creating and configuring hostpools and session hosts

- Creating and managing session host images

- Knowledge check

Technical Requirements

To complete the exercises in this book, you need to have access to a Microsoft 365 tenant. This can be attained by signing up to a trial subscription. Additionally, Azure Virtual Desktop services requires one of the following licenses:

- Microsoft 365 Business Premium

- Microsoft 365 E5/E3

- Microsoft 365 A3/A5/Student Benefits

© Shabaz Darr 2022
S. Darr, *Azure Virtual Desktop Specialist*, https://doi.org/10.1007/978-1-4842-7987-8_3

- Microsoft 365 F3

- Windows 10 Enterprise E3/E5

- Windows 10 Education A3/A5

- Windows 10 VDA per user

Implementing and Managing Networking for Azure Virtual Desktop

Azure Virtual Desktop allows organizations to host user sessions on the session hosts that are running in Azure. As discussed in Chapter 2, Microsoft manages some of the services for the customer and they deliver secure endpoints to connect end users to the session host's virtual machines.

Understanding Azure Virtual Desktop Network Connectivity

The diagram in Figure 3-1 shows a very high-level interpretation of the network connection utilized by Azure Virtual Desktop.

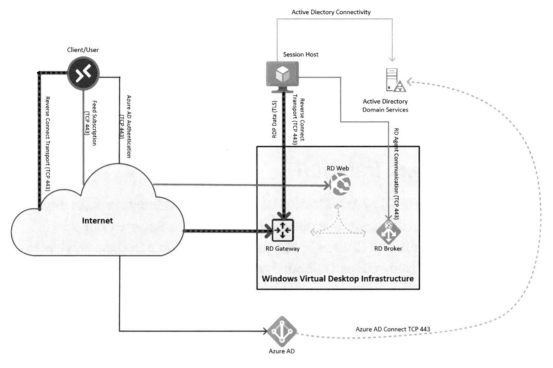

Figure 3-1. *High-level overview of network connectivity in Azure Virtual Desktop*

Figure 3-2 explains the various colors and lines.

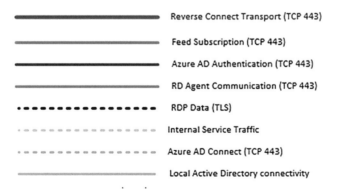

Figure 3-2. *Key for Azure Virtual Desktop network connections*

Session Connectivity

Remote Desktop Protocol (RDP) is used by Azure Virtual Desktop to deliver remote display functionality over your network connection. RDP supports multiple types of transports and has continuously been developed with every Microsoft Windows Server release.

Reverse Connect Transport

Reverse Connect is utilized by Azure Virtual Desktop when it attempts to make the remote session connection and when transporting RDP traffic. Reverse Connect Transport does not utilize a TCP listener like on-premises Remote Desktop Services to accept inbound RDP connections. Outbound connectivity to the Azure Virtual Desktop environment over HTTPS connection is used in its place.

Session Host Communication Channel

A connection is created between the Remote Desktop Agent and the Azure Virtual Desktop broker's persistent communication channel when AVD starts up. This provides a bus for a service message interchange between sessions hosts and the AVD infrastructure and this communication is layered above the Transport Layer Security (TLS) connection.

User Connection Sequence

There is a step-by-step sequence that occurs when the user attempts to make a connection to Azure Virtual Desktop. The following describes the user connection sequence:

1. A user subscribes to the Azure Virtual Desktop workspace via a supported AVD client.

2. The user is then authenticated by Azure Active Directory and a token is returned, which lists the resources available to the user.

3. The token is passed to the Azure Virtual Desktop feed subscription service by the client.

4. The token is validated by the Azure Virtual Desktop feed subscription service.

5. A list of available desktops and RemoteApps is passed back by the Azure Virtual Desktop feed subscription to the client by using a digitally signed connection configuration.

6. A set of .RDP files are utilized to store the connection configuration for each resource that is available.

7. The user then chooses the resource they want to connect to. The client then uses the associated .RDP file, makes a secure TLS 1.2 connection to the Azure Virtual Desktop gateway instance, and then passes the connection information.

8. The request is validated by the Azure Virtual Desktop gateway and a request is made to the Azure Virtual Desktop broker to coordinate the connection.

9. The session host is identified by the Azure Virtual Desktop broker, which utilizes the persistent communication channel to start the connection.

10. The TSL 1.2 connection is initiated by the Remote Desktop stack to the same AVD gateway instance that is utilized by the client.

11. Once the client and session host are connected to the gateway, unprocessed data will be transmitted between the endpoints. This will create the base reverse connect transport for the RDP.

12. The client will start the RDP handshake after the base transport is set.

In Chapter 2, you completed a lab exercise to provision a virtual network in Azure via the Admin Portal and PowerShell. The following section takes a closer look at managing connectivity.

Managing Connectivity to the Internet and On-Premises Networks

An Azure virtual network allows resources to communicate with each other in a secure manner. The default configuration is for outbound Internet communication to be allowed for all resources. For inbound communication to a specific resource, you must assign a public IP address or provision a public load balancer.

An Azure virtual network can be connected to your on-premises network using multiple options:

- **Azure Express Route:** This option creates a connection between the Azure network and your on-premises network via an ExpressRoute partner. This is a private connection where traffic does not traverse the Internet.

- **Point-to-Point VPN:** This connection is created between the Azure VNet and a specific, individual client device. This connection needs to be configured for each client device that wants to connect to the Azure network. This type of connection is more common in scenarios where you are very new to Azure, as it requires very little configuration to the existing network.

- **Site-to-Site VPN:** This connection is created between your on-premises VPN device (firewall or router) and an Azure VPN Gateway. This is deployed to your virtual network in Azure on a gateway subnet. The tunnel that is established between the gateway and on-premises devices is an encrypted tunnel over the Internet. See Figure 3-3.

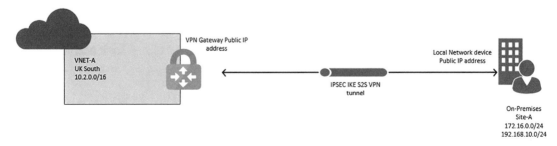

Figure 3-3. *Site-to-site VPN connectivity between Azure and on-premises*

Figure 3-3 is an logical representation of what a site-site connection between Azure and an organization's on-premises location looks like.

The following exercises walk through how to create the Azure VPN Gateway via the Admin Portal and PowerShell. You need to look at the vendor-specific documentation for your on-premises firewall/router to understand how to configure it for Azure integration.

Configure a VPN Gateway via Azure Portal

1. You can follow the steps in Chapter 2 to configure an Azure virtual network via the Admin Portal.

   You now need to create a VPN Gateway using the following settings:

   - **Name:** VNETGW1

   - **Region:** UK South

   - Gateway Type: VPN

   - **VPN type:** Route-based

   - **SKU:** VpnGw2

   - Generation: Gen 2

   - **Network:** AZ-140-vNET

   - Gateway Subnet Address Range: 10.4.1.0/27

   - **Public IP:** (Create a new one)

   - Public IP Name: VNETGW1PIP

   - Enable Active-Active Mode: Disabled

   - Configure BGP: Disabled

2. In the Azure Admin Portal, in the top Search Resources, Services, and Docs area, type ***virtual network gateway***. Click the virtual network gateway service, as shown in Figure 3-4.

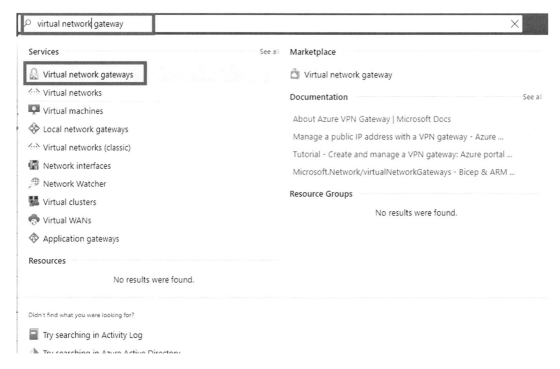

Figure 3-4. *Search for the Virtual Network Gateway service*

3. Click Create from the Virtual Network Gateway page, as shown in Figure 3-5.

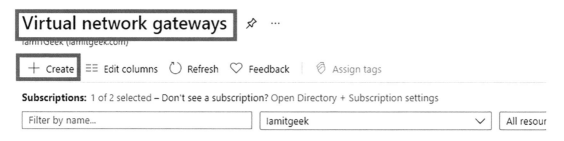

Figure 3-5. *Create a virtual network gateway*

4. Enter the relevant information, as listed in Step 1. See Figure 3-6.

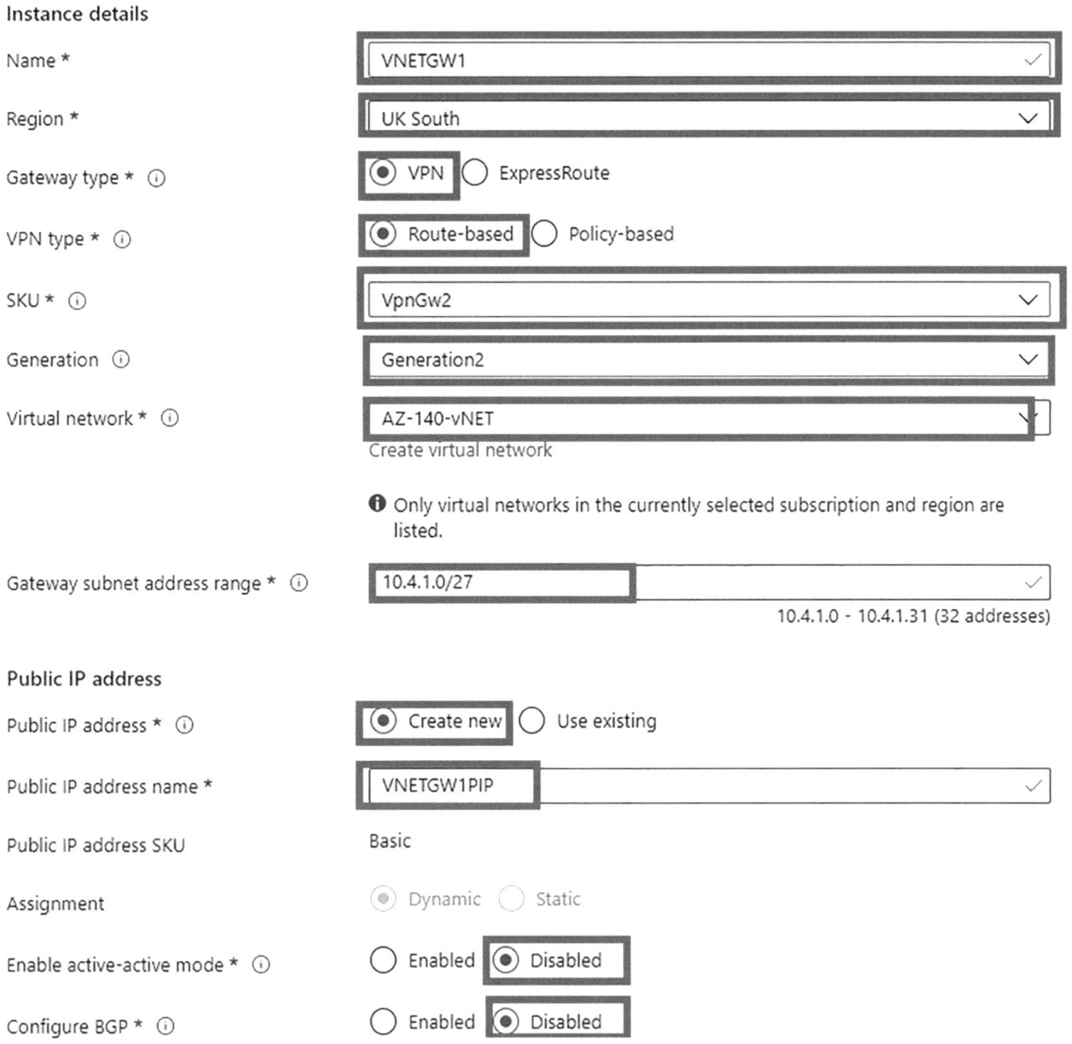

Instance details

Name *   VNETGW1

Region *   UK South

Gateway type * ⓘ   ◉ VPN   ○ ExpressRoute

VPN type * ⓘ   ◉ Route-based   ○ Policy-based

SKU * ⓘ   VpnGw2

Generation ⓘ   Generation2

Virtual network * ⓘ   AZ-140-vNET
                                    Create virtual network

                                    ❶ Only virtual networks in the currently selected subscription and region are
                                       listed.

Gateway subnet address range * ⓘ   10.4.1.0/27
                                                          10.4.1.0 - 10.4.1.31 (32 addresses)

Public IP address

Public IP address * ⓘ   ◉ Create new   ○ Use existing

Public IP address name *   VNETGW1PIP

Public IP address SKU   Basic

Assignment   ◉ Dynamic   ○ Static

Enable active-active mode * ⓘ   ○ Enabled   ◉ Disabled

Configure BGP * ⓘ   ○ Enabled   ◉ Disabled

Figure 3-6. *Input the relevant information for the instance details*

5. Add any relevant tags if you want, then complete the configuration
    by selecting Create & Review. Then click Create once the
    validation has passed.

    The next service you need to create is a local network gateway.
    This is a specific object that will represent your on-premises site
    and is used for routing. The IP address you specify during the
    configuration needs to be the same as your on-premises public IP
    address of your firewall/router.

6. Locate the Local Network Gateway service using the search box at the top of the Azure Portal and click it to go to the relevant page. See Figure 3-7.

Figure 3-7. *Search for local network gateways*

7. Click Create from the Local Network Gateway page.

8. On the Create Local Network Gateway page, enter the following information:

    - **Name:** SiteA

    - **Endpoint:** IP address

    - **IP Address:** (This should be the public IP address for on-premises firewall/router.)

    - **Address Space:** (These should be the private address ranges in your on-premises network that you want to route to Azure.)

    - Configure BGP Settings: Unticked

    - **Subscription:** (Your trial subscription.)

- **Resource Group:** (The resource group you created in Chapter 2. This example uses a different resource group.)

- **Location:** UK South

Click Create once you have entered all the relevant information. See Figure 3-8.

Figure 3-8. *Configuring a local network gateway*

Now that you have configured the VPN Gateway and local gateway in Azure, you would need to configure your on-premises network device (firewall or router). You need to have the following information when configuring your on-premises VPN device:

- **A Shared Key:** This is specified when the site-to-site connection is created. (This example uses a basic shared key.)

- **Public IP Address:** This is the public IP address of your virtual network gateway; you can get this from the Azure Portal or obtain it from PowerShell or CLI.

You can also download a configuration script, depending on the make and model of your on-premises device.

The final configuration step before being able to test and verify your site-to-site connection is to create a VPN connection. The following lab exercise demonstrates how you can complete this process using the following settings:

- Local Network Gateway: SiteA

- Connection Name: VNetAtoSiteA

- **Shared Key:** (This is the shared key you set up in the earlier step when configuring your on-premises device.)

9. Navigate to the Virtual Network Gateway by choosing VNET ➤ Overview ➤ Connected Devices ➤ your gateway. See Figure 3-9.

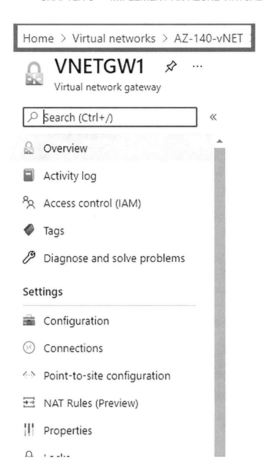

Figure 3-9. *Navigate to the Virtual Network Gateway window*

10. On this page, you need to click the Connections tab and then choose +Add, as shown in Figure 3-10.

Figure 3-10. *Add a connection to the VPN Gateway*

11. Enter the relevant details (see Figure 3-11):

- **Name:** VnetAtoSiteA

- **Connection Type:** Site-to-site (IPSec)

- Virtual Network Gateway: VNETGW1

- Local Network Gateway: SiteA

- **Shared key (PSK):** (This is the same as what you set up on your on-premises device.)

- Use Azure Private IP Address: Unticked

- Enable BGP: Unticked

- IKE Protocol: IKEv2

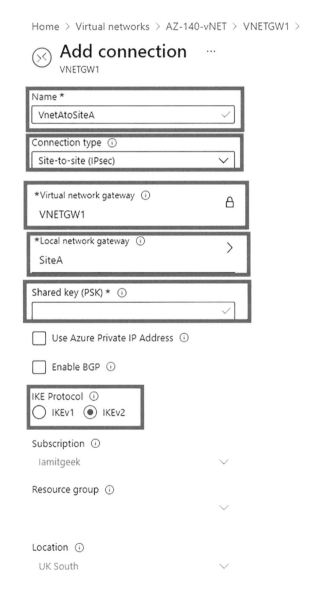

Figure 3-11. *Configure the VPN connection*

You can then verify that it's connected by looking at the status.

Configuring a VPN Connection via PowerShell

Before you can complete this exercise, you need to ensure you have already completed the steps in Chapter 2 and created a resource group and a virtual network.

You need to connect to Azure via PowerShell. Follow the instructions in this link to do so: https://docs.microsoft.com/en-us/powershell/azure/authenticate-azureps?view=azps-6.4.0.

1. First set the variables with the cmdlets shown in Figure 3-12.

```
PS C:\WINDOWS\system32> $vnet = Get-AzVirtualNetwork -ResourceGroupName ITGEEKRG01 -Name "AZ-140-vNET"
```

Figure 3-12. *Set the network and resource group variables*

2. Use the cmdlet shown in Figure 3-13 to create the gateway subnet.

```
PS C:\WINDOWS\system32> Add-AzVirtualNetworkSubnetConfig -Name 'GatewaySubnet' -AddressPrefix 10.4.2.0/27 -VirtualNetwork $vnet
```

Figure 3-13. *Create the gateway subnet cmdlet*

3. You now need to set the configuration in PowerShell using the cmdlet shown in Figure 3-14.

```
PS C:\WINDOWS\system32> Set-AzVirtualNetwork -VirtualNetwork $vnet
```

Figure 3-14. *Set the configuration cmdlet*

Configure the Local Gateway via PowerShell

For the following exercise, use these values:

- The GatewayIPAddress is the on-premises VPN device IP address

- The AddressPrefix is the on-premises private address space

4. The cmdlets shown in Figure 3-15 will add the local gateway with a single on-premises IP address.

```
PS C:\WINDOWS\system32> New-AzLocalNetworkGateway -Name SiteA -ResourceGroupName ITGEEKRG01 `
>> -Location 'UK South' -GatewayIpAddress '              ' -AddressPrefix
```

Figure 3-15. *Add a local gateway with a single public IP address and private IP address range.*

> You need to request a public IP address for the VPN Gateway. Note that this only supports dynamic public IP addresses at the moment, so you are unable to request a public, static IP address.

5. Enter the cmdlet shown in Figure 3-16 to request a public IP address. It will be assigned to your VPN Gateway.

```
PS C:\WINDOWS\system32> $gwpip= New-AzPublicIpAddress -Name VNetAGWPIP -ResourceGroupName IAMITGEEKRG01 -Location 'UK West' -AllocationMethod Dynamic
```

Figure 3-16. *Request a public IP for the VPN Gateway*

> Once the public IP address has been requested, you need to create the gateway IP address configuration. This defines the subnet (GatewaySubnet) and the public IP that will be utilized.

6. The example cmdlets shown in Figures 3-17 through 3-19 create the gateway configuration.

```
PS C:\WINDOWS\system32> $vnet = Get-AzVirtualNetwork -Name "AZ-140-vNET" -ResourceGroupName ITGEEKRG01
```

Figure 3-17. *Set the $vnet variable to create the gateway configuration*

```
PS C:\WINDOWS\system32> $subnet = Get-AzVirtualNetworkSubnetConfig -Name 'GatewaySubnet' -VirtualNetwork $vnet
```

Figure 3-18. *Set the $subnet variable to create the gateway subnet*

```
PS C:\WINDOWS\system32> $gwipconfig = New-AzVirtualNetworkGatewayIpConfig -Name gwipconfig1 -SubnetId $subnet.Id -PublicIpAddressId $gwpip.Id
```

Figure 3-19. *Gateway configuration cmdlet*

> Once the configuration has been set, you need to create the VPN Gateway. Note the following values:

- -GatewayType for the site-to-site configuration will be VPN. This setting is specific to the type of VPN you want to configure. Another example setting for this could be ExpressRoute.

- -VpnType will be RouteBased. This setting has another option that can be set to PolicyBased, which is compatible with more legacy on-premises VPN devices.

- -GatewaySku is for the gateway SKU you want to use. In this example, we set this to VpnGw1. For more information about Gateway SKUs, see `https://docs.microsoft.com/en-us/azure/vpn-gateway/vpn-gateway-about-vpn-gateway-settings#gwsku`.

7. The cmdlet shown in Figure 3-20 will configure the VPN Gateway.

```
PS C:\WINDOWS\system32> New-AzVirtualNetworkGateway -Name VNet1GW -ResourceGroupName ITGEEKRG01 `
>> -Location 'UK South' -IpConfigurations $gwipconfig -GatewayType Vpn `
>> -VpnType RouteBased -GatewaySku VpnGw1
```

Figure 3-20. *Configure the VPN Gateway*

Once the VPN Gateway is configured, you should configure your on-premises VPN device the same way you did when completing the steps via the Azure Portal. After you have completed the step, you can now create the VPN connection via PowerShell.

8. The cmdlets shown in Figures 3-21 and 3-22 will set the variables for the VPN connection configuration.

```
PS C:\WINDOWS\system32> $gateway1 = Get-AzVirtualNetworkGateway -Name VNet1GW -ResourceGroupName ITGEEKRG01
```

Figure 3-21. *Set the $gateway1 variable cmdlet*

```
PS C:\WINDOWS\system32> $local = Get-AzLocalNetworkGateway -Name SiteA -ResourceGroupName ITGEEKRG01
```

Figure 3-22. *Set the $local gateway variable cmdlet*

9. The cmdlet shown in Figure 3-23 will utilize these variables to configure the connection.

```
PS C:\WINDOWS\system32> New-AzVirtualNetworkGatewayConnection -Name VNetAtoSiteA -ResourceGroupName ITGEEKRG01 `
>> -Location 'UK South' -VirtualNetworkGateway1 $gateway1 -LocalNetworkGateway2 $local `
>> -ConnectionType IPsec -RoutingWeight 10 -SharedKey '123ABC'
```

Figure 3-23. *Configure the connection via PowerShell*

In this section, we added to the initial virtual network configuration from Chapter 2 and configured a virtual network gateway, a local network gateway, and a VPN connection to an on-premises VPN device via the Azure Portal and PowerShell. The next section looks at adding to the existing storage account service by implementing and managing storage for Azure Virtual Desktop.

Implementing and Managing Storage for Azure Virtual Desktop

Azure Virtual Desktop utilizes Azure File shares within an Azure Storage account to manage user profiles and specific application containerization. FSLogix profile containers are recommended as a user profile service, and they integrate with Azure Files.

The FSLogix solution enables you to manage non-persistent Windows environments. You can do the following:

- Preserve user settings in non-persistent environments

- Reduce login times for non-persistent environments

- Optimize file input/output (I/O)

- Provide a local profile experience for users

- Enable simple app and image management

A user's profile includes configuration information like desktop settings, persistent network connections, and app settings. This profile is a barrier between the data for the user and the OS.

FSLogix profiles can be used to:

- Segregate user profiles from VMs

- Persist the profiles as user-assigned virtual disks in Azure Storage, Azure NetApp files, or Storage Spaces Direct

- Attach profiles dynamically to a user

FSLogix works in a similar way to traditional roaming profiles, and it stores the user profile in a single container. When the user logs in to Azure Virtual Desktop, this container is dynamically attached to the user's session by using virtual hard disks (VHD) and Hyper-V Virtual Hard disks (VHDX). The user profile is then accessible and appears as a local profile.

Before you configure FSLogix, you need to create an Azure File share in your storage account. In Chapter 2, you created a premium storage account that will enable you to provision the Azure File share. Once you have provisioned the share, you need to domain-join the share to your Active Directory domain, which will enable you to provision the required security permissions.

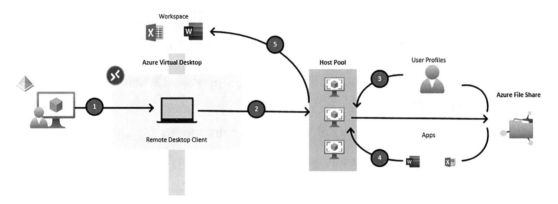

Figure 3-24. *Process of getting a user profile*

Figure 3-24 displays the process that is undertaken when obtaining a user profile after the user logs in to the Desktop client. The following steps explain this process in more detail:

1. The end user logs in to the remote desktop client with their Azure AD credentials (email address).

2. The user is logged in/assigned to a session host (VM).

3. The session host obtains the user's profile from the Azure File share.

4. If you have MSIX app attach configured (see Chapter 5), applications are dynamically sent to the VMs. FSLogix storage concepts are used in this scenario.

5. The end user's Azure Virtual Desktop workspace is filled with the applications that have been assigned to them or their session desktop.

This section introduced FSLogix and explained how it can integrate with Azure Storage accounts. The next section looks at how to create FSLogix profiles for Azure Virtual Desktop.

Creating FSLogix Profiles for Azure Virtual Desktops

FSLogix requires an Azure Storage account so you can use it to segregate user profiles from the session hosts. We implemented this in Chapter 2, so the following lab exercises will walk through how to configure Azure Files with an Azure Active Directory Domain Services (Azure AD DS). These steps are almost identical to when integrating with Active Directory Domain Services (on-premises), with the only difference being the Enable Azure Active Directory Authentication steps. We point out those differences in this section.

Enable Azure Active Directory Authentication

This lab exercise covers how to enable authentication for Azure File shares with Azure AD DS. If you have a domain controller on-premises, you are required to register the storage account with AD DS, which will then allow you to set domain properties on the storage account.

The AzFilesHybrid Azure PowerShell module is utilized on a domain-joined machine to complete this process. You can perform the Join-AzStorageAccountForAuth cmdlet to complete the same for an offline domain join for the Azure Storage account. You can find more information at `https://docs.microsoft.com/en-us/azure/storage/files/storage-files-identity-ad-ds-enable`.

1. In the Azure Portal, navigate to the storage account you set up in Chapter 2.

2. In the Storage account, navigate to Data Storage ➤ File Shares, as shown in Figure 3-25.

≡ Overview

▤ Activity log

◆ Tags

🔧 Diagnose and solve problems

👥 Access Control (IAM)

📦 Data migration

🗄 Storage browser (preview)

Data storage

🗂 File shares

Security + networking

Figure 3-25. *Navigate to the File Shares pane*

3. On the File Shares page, click the Not Configured link next to Active Directory. See Figure 3-26.

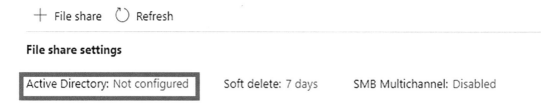

＋ File share ↻ Refresh

File share settings

Active Directory: Not configured   Soft delete: 7 days   SMB Multichannel: Disabled

Figure 3-26. *Select the Active Directory: Not Configured option*

4. On the Storage Account Active Directory page, you will see two options below the "Step 1: Enable an Active Directory Source"— Active Directory and Azure Active Directory Domain Services. Click Set Up under Active Directory Domain Services. See Figure 3-27.

Figure 3-27. *Azure Active Directory Domain Service Set Up option*

5. In the Set Up Azure AD DS window, tick the box next to the Enable
    Azure Active Directory Domain Services (Azure AD DS) For This
    File Share option, as shown in Figure 3-28.

Figure 3-28. *Enable Azure AD DS integration with Azure Storage account*

Once you have saved this setting, the lab is complete. In Figure 3-28, you will see a
warning at the bottom that is explains that you need to ensure you have enabled Azure
AD Domain Services in your tenant before completing the storage account integration.
You can find steps for configuring Azure AD Domain Services at `https://docs.`
`microsoft.com/en-us/azure/active-directory-domain-services/tutorial-create-`
`instance`.

Now that you have joined the Azure Storage account to an Azure AD DS domain, you
need to assign the relevant roles to access the storage data for both users and AAD DC
Administrator groups.

Assign a Role to AAD DC Administrators

The following lab exercise gives the administrators the capability to edit NTFS permissions by assigning a role with elevated contributor access to the file share.

1.   Navigate to the storage account you created in Chapter 2 and select the Access Control (IAM) option in the left pane menu. See Figure 3-29.

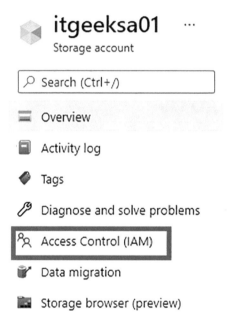

Figure 3-29. Navigate to Access Control (IAM) for the storage account

2.   Click +Add and then Add Role Assignment, as shown in Figure 3-30.

Figure 3-30. Add a role assignment

3. In the Add Role Assignment window, select Storage File Data SMB Elevated Contributor for the role.

4. Under Assign Access, ensure you have selected User, group, or Service Principal. Under the Select option, click the AAD DC Administrators group. See Figure 3-31.

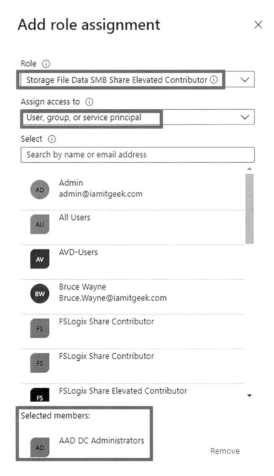

Figure 3-31. *Add the Storage File Data SMB Elevated Contributor role to the AA DC Administrators group*

5. Click Save.

Assign a Role to Non-Administrator Azure Virtual Desktop Users

In the following lab exercise, you will assign users a contributor level role, which will grant them permissions to read and write file data in the file share. This will allow users to access the user profile virtual desks that are stored in the file share.

1. Follow Steps 1 and 2 in the previous exercise to navigate to the Add Role Assignment page.

2. Under the Role option, select Storage File Data SMB Share Contributor.

3. Under the Assign Access To option, ensure that Azure AD User, Group, Or Service Principal is selected.

4. You now have the option to either add users individually or add the users to a security group and add that group to the role assignment. It is a recommended practice to add users to a group and then to the role assignment. See Figure 3-32.

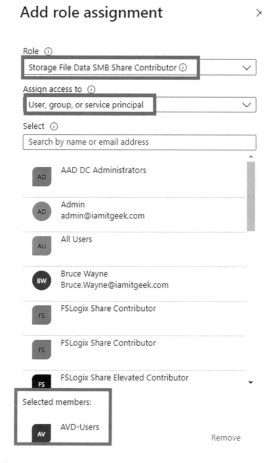

Figure 3-32. *Add role assignment for Azure Virtual Desktop user permissions to the file share*

    5.   Click Save.

Create a File Share to Store the User Profile Virtual Disks

The following lab exercise walks through how to create a file share within the Azure Storage account.

    1.   Navigate to the Azure Storage account.

    2.   Under Data Storage, choose File Shares. See Figure 3-33.

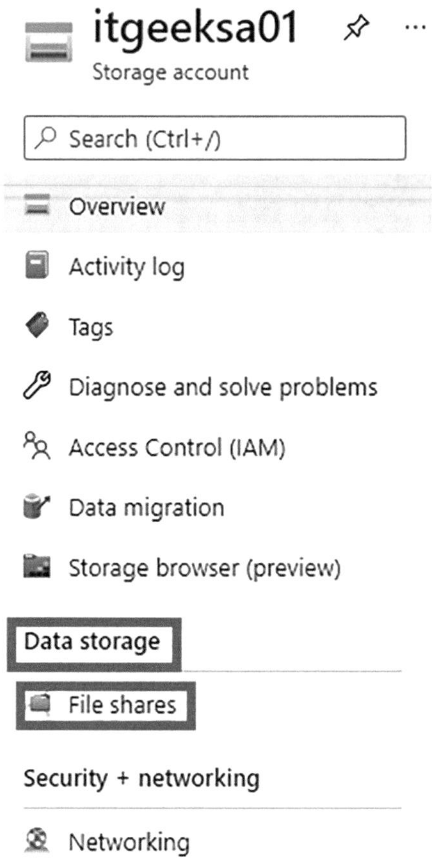

itgeeksa01
Storage account
Search (Ctrl+/)
Overview
Activity log
Tags
Diagnose and solve problems
Access Control (IAM)
Data migration
Storage browser (preview)
Data storage
File shares
Security + networking
Networking

Figure 3-33. *Navigate to file shares or to the Azure Storage account*

3. Click + File Share, as shown in Figure 3-34.

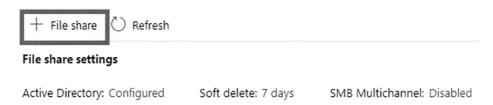

File share
Refresh
File share settings
Active Directory: Configured
Soft delete: 7 days
SMB Multichannel: Disabled

Figure 3-34. *Select + File share*

4. Enter the following fields in the New Share windows (see
    Figure 3-35):

    - **Name**: Enter a relevant name.

    - **Provisioned Capacity:** Enter the size you want the file share to
      be in GB.

    - **Protocol:** You can use SMB or NFS. This example uses SMB.

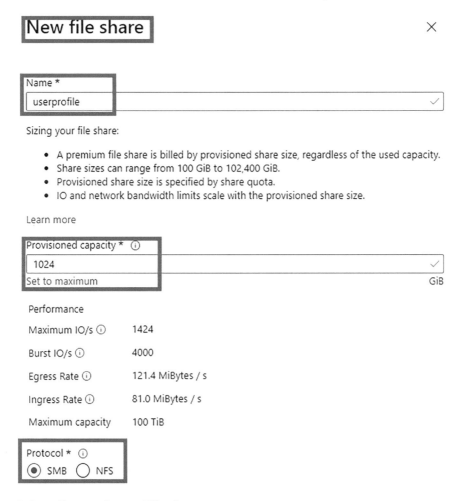

Figure 3-35. *Create Azure File share*

5. Click Create.

Once the file share is configured, you need to get both the storage account access
keys and the file share path.

Get the Storage Account Access Keys

In this lab exercise, you will obtain the storage account access keys.

1. Choose Azure Storage Account ➤ Security + Networking ➤ Access Keys, as shown in Figure 3-36.

Figure 3-36. *Navigate to Access Keys*

2. Copy one of the key values to a notepad for later use. You can click Show Keys at the top of the window to show the full key. See Figure 3-37.

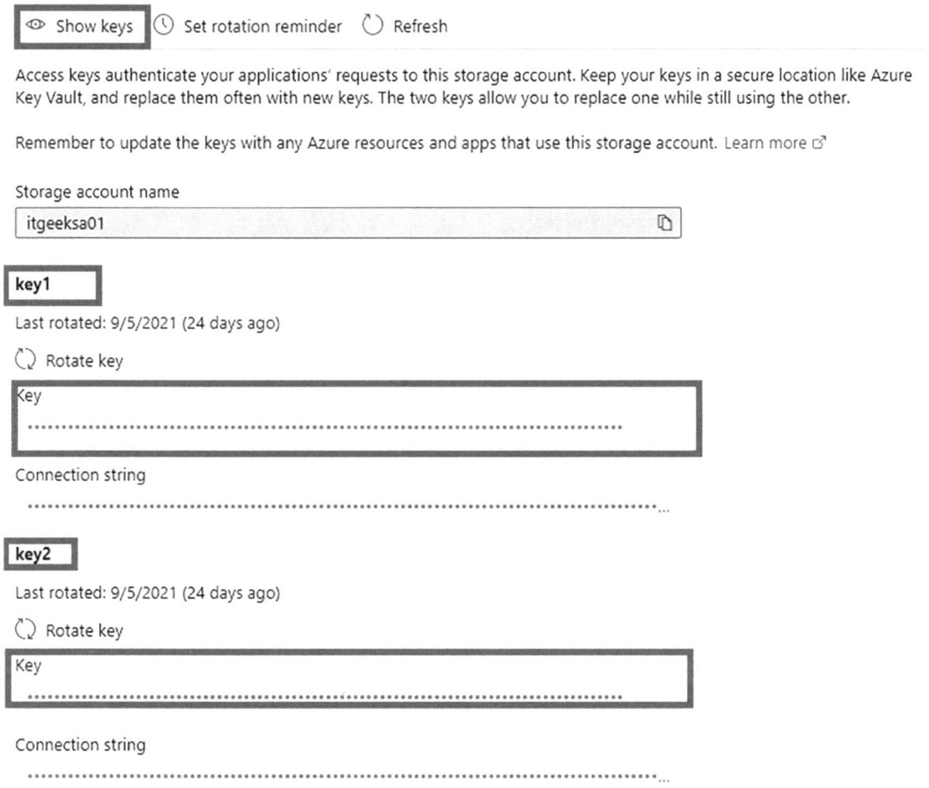

👁 Show keys   🕐 Set rotation reminder   ↻ Refresh

Access keys authenticate your applications' requests to this storage account. Keep your keys in a secure location like Azure Key Vault, and replace them often with new keys. The two keys allow you to replace one while still using the other.

Remember to update the keys with any Azure resources and apps that use this storage account. Learn more ⌕

Storage account name

```
itgeeksa01                                                    🗋
```

key1

Last rotated: 9/5/2021 (24 days ago)

↻ Rotate key

```
Key
.................................................................
```

Connection string
....

key2

Last rotated: 9/5/2021 (24 days ago)

↻ Rotate key

```
Key
.................................................................
```

Connection string
....

Figure 3-37. *Obtaining access keys for storage account*

Get a File Path Share

In this lab exercise, you obtain the file share path.

1. Choose Azure Storage Account ➤ Data Storage ➤ File Shares and click the file share you created in Chapter 2.

2. Under Settings, choose Properties. See Figure 3-38.

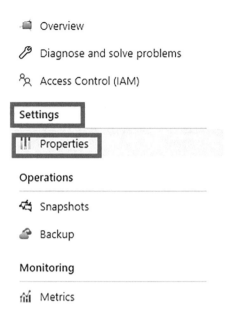

Figure 3-38. *Navigate to the file share properties*

3. Copy the URL and convert it from an HTTP path to an SMB path
    for later use; see Figure 3-39.

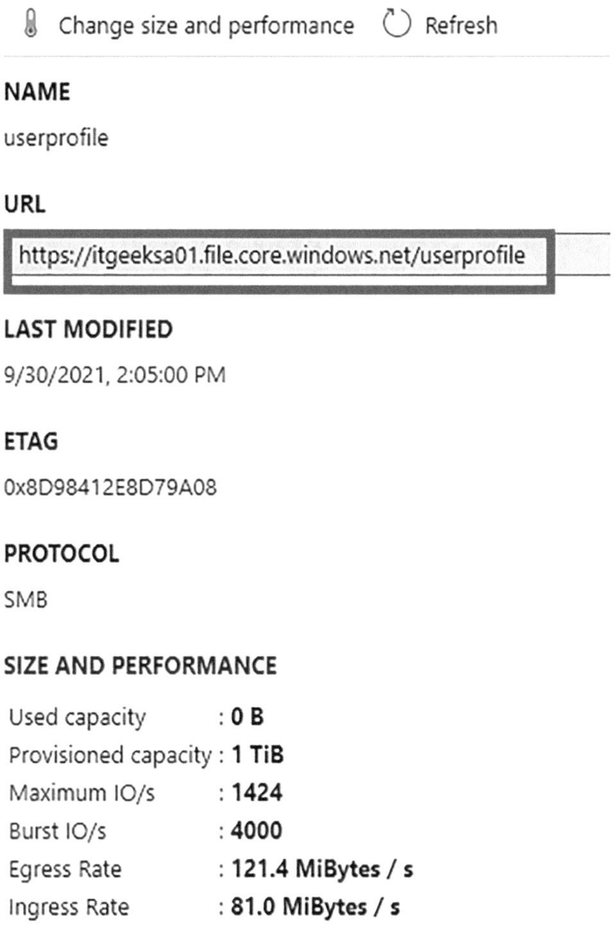

🌡 Change size and performance   ↻ Refresh

NAME
userprofile

URL
https://itgeeksa01.file.core.windows.net/userprofile

LAST MODIFIED
9/30/2021, 2:05:00 PM

ETAG
0x8D98412E8D79A08

PROTOCOL
SMB

SIZE AND PERFORMANCE
Used capacity   : **0 B**
Provisioned capacity : **1 TiB**
Maximum IO/s   : **1424**
Burst IO/s   : **4000**
Egress Rate   : **121.4 MiBytes / s**
Ingress Rate   : **81.0 MiBytes / s**

Figure 3-39. *Copy the HTTP URL*

In this section, you completed lab exercises to configure the Azure Storage account with Azure AD DS, configured an Azure File share, configured permissions, and got both the storage key and the share file path. We do not discuss how to configure FSLogix on session hosts.

At present, virtual machines that are created by utilizing the Azure gallery images will have FSLogix already installed. However, the following steps are necessary for the scenario in which you use non-gallery images and are required to manually install the FSLogix software.

Install the FSLogix Software for Non-Gallery Images

The following steps outline what you are required to do to install the FSLogix software on non-gallery images.

1. Download the FSLogix agent on to each VM that is registered to an existing hostpool. Download the software from `https://docs.microsoft.com/en-us/fslogix/install-ht`.

2. Once the contents of the ZIP file are extracted, navigate to either `\Win32\Release` or `\X64\Release` (depending on the OS of the VM).

3. Install the FSLogixAppsSetup setup file on each VM to install the FSLogix agent.

   Now you understand how to install FSLogix on non-gallery VMs that are registered to a hostpool. In the next section, you will complete a lab exercise to configure FSLogix.

Configure FSLogix

The following lab exercise walks through how to configure FSLogix on hostpool-registered virtual machines.

1. On the Windows virtual machine, navigate to the Start menu. Type **Regedit** and then right-click and choose Run as Administrator.

2. Navigate to `Computer\HKEY_LOCAL_MACHINE\software\FSLogix`, as shown in Figure 3-40.

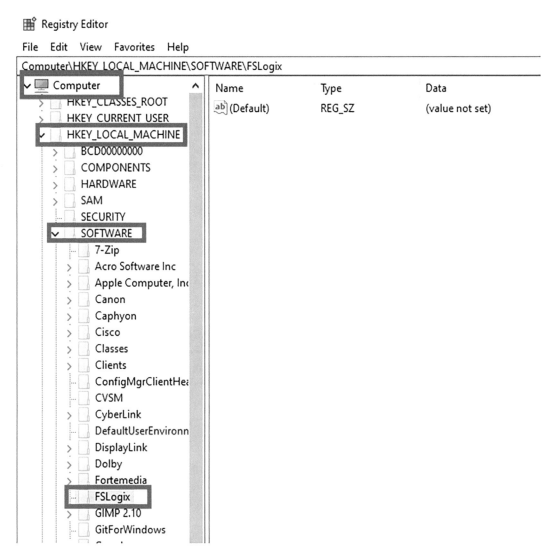

Figure 3-40. *Navigate to the FSLogix registry key*

3. Right-click the FSLogix key and create a new key called Profiles.
   See Figure 3-41.

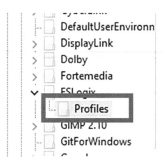

Figure 3-41. *Create the Profiles key*

4. Create the data type entries outlined in Table 3-1 under the
   Profiles key.

Table 3-1. *Registry Entries for the Profiles Key*

Type	Name	Data/Value
DWORD	Enabled	1
Multi-String Value	VHDLocations	Azure File Share location

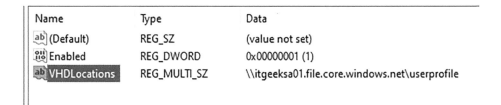

Figure 3-42. *Registry entries for user profiles*

5. Open a command prompt with elevated permissions.

6. Run the command shown in Figure 3-42. Note that you may
   need to replace the values with your own specific details. In my
   example, I used the following:

- **SMB File share path:** `\\itgeeksa01.file.core.windows.net\userprofile`

- Storage Account: `itgeeksa01`

- **Access keys:** `KJ26KewgXZ2zqiOR2STPDmhyi7+mnpcCBJHyrguoxIPS Fq4U6NbAHVxEYcHCQyLGluhrLztYgVSidH7enVeJ7g==`

- **Users Azure UPN:** `shabaz@iamitgeek.com`

```
C:\WINDOWS\system32>net use Z: "\\itgeeksa01.file.core.windows.net\userprofile" /u:Azure\itgeeksa01 KJ26KewgXZ2zqiOR2STP
Dmhyi7+mnpcCBJHyrguoxIPSFq4U6NbAHVxEYcHCQyLGluhrLztYgVSidH7enVeJ7g==
```

Figure 3-43. *Map the drive to the Azure File share in an elevated command prompt*

```
C:\WINDOWS\system32>Icacls Z: /grant "shabaz@iamitgeek.com":(f)
```

Figure 3-44. *Grant the UPN the relevant permissions*

In this section, you configured FSLogix on the Windows VMs that are registered to an existing hostpool. In the final step, you create the FSLogix profile.

Create the FSLogix Profile

These two steps must be completed to create the FSLogix profile and ensure that the VM does not already have a user's profile created on it.

1. Open an Internet browser on the VM and navigate to `https://aka.ms/wvdwebarm`.

2. Log in to a VM that you have not signed into yet.

Note that the initial login may take longer than usual, as it is creating the virtual disk file for the first time.

This section configured the storage account created in Chapter 2, created an Azure File share, configured FSLogix, and configured the profile disks. In the next section, you create and configure hostpools and session hosts.

Creating and Configuring Hostpools and Session Hosts

In this section, we are going to discuss creating and configuring hostpools and sessions hosts as well as complete some lab exercises.

After you have deployed all the underlying infrastructure, including the network and storage, and made customizations to your Windows 10 image (See the section "Creating and Configuring Session Host Images"), you are ready to create a hostpool, specify your session host virtual machines, and create your workspace.

Hostpools

A *hostpool* is a set of virtual machines known as session hosts. You can deploy two different types of hostpools:

- *Pooled hostpool:* This type of hostpool allows you to deploy a multi-session environment in which several end users can log in to the virtual machine and share the resources. There are only specific versions of Windows 10 that support multi-session, including Windows 10 Enterprise Multi-session, which is only available from the Azure image gallery.

- *Personal hostpool:* This type of hostpool is more suited for a scenario in which you require each user to have their own virtual machine and not share resources.

When configuring the pooled hostpool type, two types of load-balancing algorithms can be configured:

- *Breadth-first:* This is generally the default configuration and is for non-persistent hostpools. This algorithm shares the new user sessions across all the session hosts that are available in the hostpool. You can set a maximum session limit per session host.

- *Depth-first:* This algorithm shares new user sessions to a session host that is available that has the greatest number of connections, but that has not yet reached its limit. Once it reaches its limit, it distributes to the next session host with the greatest number of connections. You must set a maximum session limit when choosing this algorithm.

Application Groups

An application group allows you to group RemoteApps and resources, then assign them to specific users or groups. There are two types of application groups:

- *RemoteApp:* A RemoteApp allows users to access applications that have been published by an administrator to the application group. Multiple RemoteApp groups can be created, which will enable you to meet different requirements/scenarios.

- *Remote Desktop:* This is where an end user accesses a full virtual desktop. This is automatically created by default when you create the hostpool and is called Desktop Application Group.

Workspaces

A *workspace* is a logical container in which all of the application groups are stored within Azure Virtual Desktop. When a user logs in to Azure Virtual Desktop via the remote desktop app, they are in fact logging in to the workspace, with either or both a desktop or applications published for them to use. See Figure 3-45.

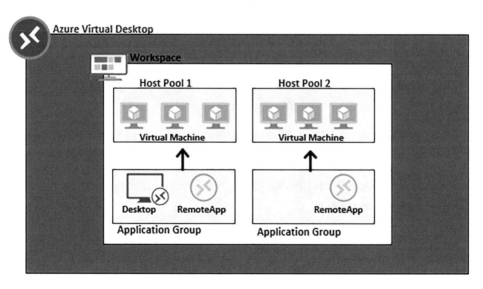

Figure 3-45. *Azure Virtual Desktop workspace*

Virtual Machines

You can create new virtual machines or register existing ones to your hostpool. A hostpool can have a maximum of 159 virtual machines when you configure and deploy your first one. More VMs can be deployed after the initial hostpool has been deployed, but you need to check the Azure VM and API limits for your specific resource group and subscription, as there can also be an 800-Azure-resource per deployment limit as well.

Image Types

Session host images are covered later in this chapter; however as a quick overview, there are two image types from which you can chose when creating your virtual machine for your hostpool:

- *Gallery:* You can select one of the recommended images from the gallery drop-down menu. For example, you can choose Windows 10 Enterprise Multi-Session. You can also browse all images and disks, which will allow you to select another image from the Azure gallery, or select an image you have customized and uploaded yourself.

- *Storage blob:* This option is normally utilized when you have an image you are using on-premises that you uploaded. You have some additional options when you select this image type:

  - **Image URI:** You enter an URL to the location of a generalized VHD from the Azure Storage account.

  - **Use Managed Disks:** Microsoft recommends that you select Yes for this option.

  - **Storage Account:** Choose the Azure Storage account where the image is stored.

The following lab exercise walks through creating a hostpool via the Azure Portal and PowerShell.

Creating a Hostpool by Utilizing the Azure Portal

1. Sign in to https://portal.azure.com with your global admin credentials.

2. Navigate to the Azure Virtual Desktop service by utilizing the search function at the top of the window, as shown in Figure 3-46.

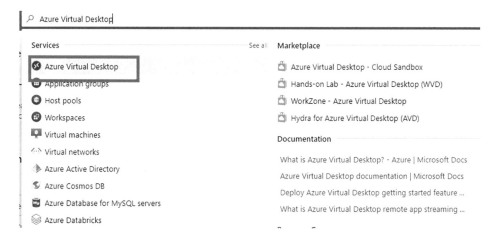

Figure 3-46. *Navigate to the Azure Virtual Desktop service in the Azure Portal*

3. Click Create a Host Pool in the middle of the page, as shown in Figure 3-47.

Figure 3-47. *Create a hostpool*

4. On the Basics tab, enter the following information and click Next
    (see Figure 3-48):

    - **Subscription ID:** This is the name of your trial subscription.

    - **Resource Group:** The resource group you created in Chapter 2.

    - **Host Pool Name:** Enter the name you want to give your hostpool.

    - **Location:** Select the location for your hostpool metadata.

    - **Validation Environment:** This allows you to test the deployment
      before going into production. Select Yes or No.

    - **Host Pool Type:** You have two options, Personal or Pooled. This
      example creates a pooled host pool.

    - **Load Balancing Algorithm:** This example uses breadth-first.

    - **Max Session Limit:** We will set this to 5 in this example.

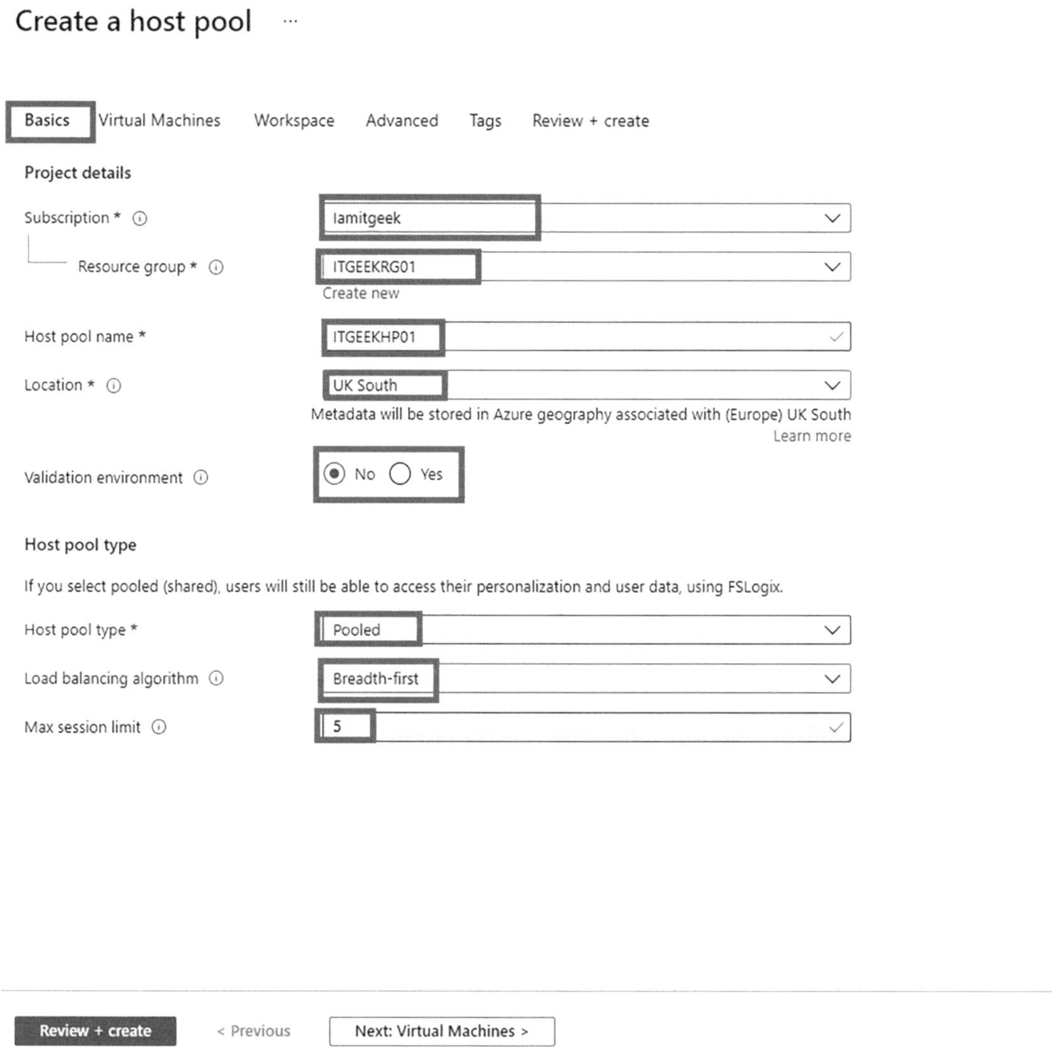

Create a host pool ⋯

Basics | Virtual Machines | Workspace | Advanced | Tags | Review + create

Project details

Subscription * ⓘ

    Iamitgeek

Resource group * ⓘ

    ITGEEKRG01
    Create new

Host pool name *

    ITGEEKHP01

Location * ⓘ

    UK South

Metadata will be stored in Azure geography associated with (Europe) UK South
Learn more

Validation environment ⓘ

    ⦿ No ◯ Yes

Host pool type

If you select pooled (shared), users will still be able to access their personalization and user data, using FSLogix.

Host pool type *

    Pooled

Load balancing algorithm ⓘ

    Breadth-first

Max session limit ⓘ

    5

Review + create   < Previous   Next: Virtual Machines >

Figure 3-48. *Basics tab when creating a hostpool*

5. On the Virtual Machine tab, if you want to add virtual machines later, leave the No option selected. In this example we want to add them now, so click Yes.

6. Complete the fields as follows and then click Next (see Figures 3-49 and 3-50):

- **Resource Group:** The resource group you created in Chapter 2.

- **Name Prefix:** This is the naming convention for your virtual machines that are registered to your hostpool. The name you choose will automatically be assigned -X, where the X is unique number starting with 0. For example, if you have five virtual machines, they will have -0, -1, -2, -3, and -4 at the end of the name you choose.

- **Virtual Machine Location:** The Azure location where you want to store the VMs.

- **Availability Options:** Azure offers a range of availability options for managing availability and resiliency. You can choose from Availability Zone or Availability Set. In this example, we will leave it as the default, which is Availability Zone.

- **Availability Zone:** Select the number of the availability zone in which to deploy your Azure resources.

- **Image Type:** You can choose from Gallery and Storage Blob. In this example, we use Gallery.

- **Image:** You have the choice of selecting an image from the Azure Gallery or browsing to an image you uploaded. In this example we choose Windows 10 Enterprise Multi-Session, Version 20H2 + Microsoft 365 Apps (GEN2).

- **Virtual Machine Size:** This choice depends on how you have sized your virtual machines. In this example, we select Standard B2ms.

- **Number of VMs:** This is the number of virtual machines you want to create as part of your hostpool.

- **OS Disk Type:** You can choose Standard SSD, Standard HDD, or Premium SSD. In this example, we choose Premium SSD.

- **Boot Diagnostics:** Select the recommended Enable with Managed Storage account.

- **Virtual Network:** Select the VNet you created in Chapter 2.

- **Subnet:** Select the subnet you created in Chapter 2.

- **Network Security Groups:** You can select Basic, None, or Advanced.

- **Public Inbound Ports:** Leave this set to No unless you have a specific requirement.

- **Domain Join:** Choose if you want to use Active Directory or Azure AD DS. This example uses Active Directory, which requires you to enter the domain admin credentials for the domain join.

- **Virtual Machine Admin:** Enter the credentials you want to set as the local administrator on the new virtual machines.

- **Post Update Custom Configuration:** If you have any custom ARM templates for any post deployment configuration, you can enter the URL in this section.

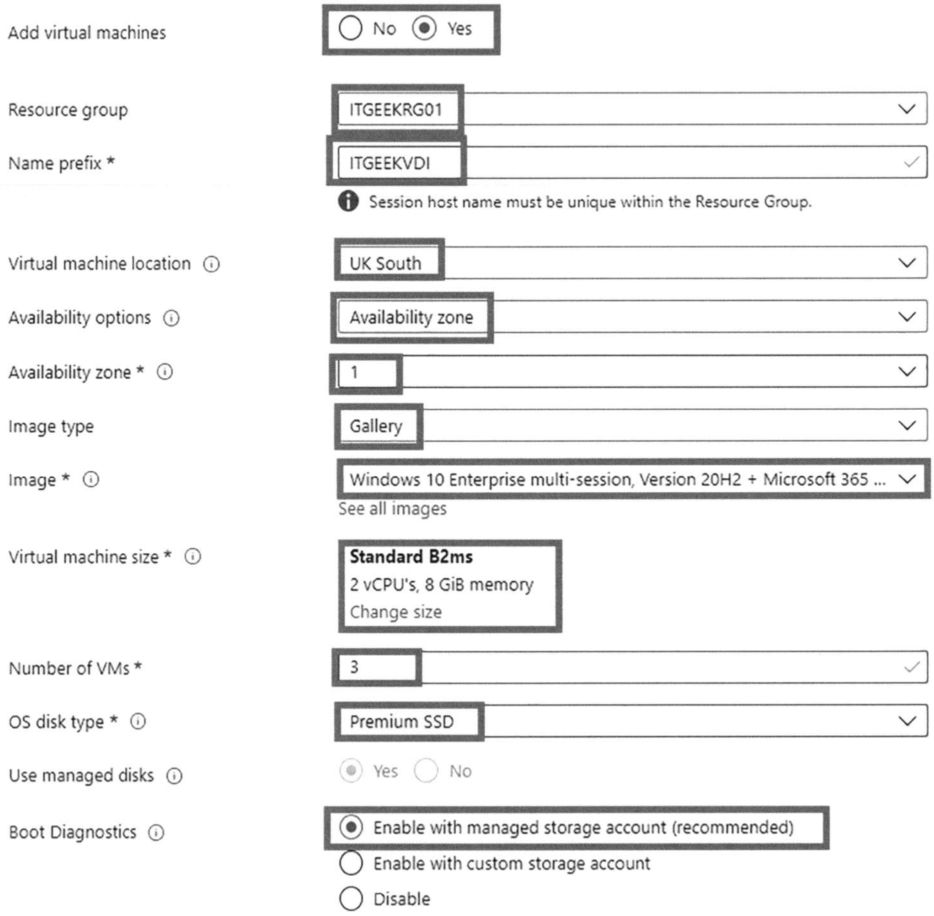

Add virtual machines	◯ No ⦿ Yes
Resource group	ITGEEKRG01 ⌄
Name prefix *	ITGEEKVDI

ⓘ Session host name must be unique within the Resource Group.

Virtual machine location ⓘ	UK South ⌄
Availability options ⓘ	Availability zone ⌄
Availability zone * ⓘ	1 ⌄
Image type	Gallery ⌄
Image * ⓘ	Windows 10 Enterprise multi-session, Version 20H2 + Microsoft 365 ... ⌄
	See all images
Virtual machine size * ⓘ	**Standard B2ms** 2 vCPU's, 8 GiB memory Change size
Number of VMs *	3
OS disk type * ⓘ	Premium SSD ⌄
Use managed disks ⓘ	⦿ Yes ◯ No
Boot Diagnostics ⓘ	⦿ Enable with managed storage account (recommended) ◯ Enable with custom storage account ◯ Disable

Figure 3-49. *Enter the Virtual Machine details, part 1*

Virtual network * ⓘ	AZ-140-vNET ⌄
Subnet ⓘ	default (10.4.0.0/24) ⌄
Network security group ⓘ	Basic ⌄
Public inbound ports ⓘ	○ Yes ● No
Inbound ports to allow	Select one or more ports ⌄
	❶ All traffic from the internet will be blocked by default.

Domain to join

Select which directory you would like to join	Azure Active Directory ⌄
Enroll VM with Intune ⓘ	● Yes ○ No

Virtual Machine Administrator account

Username * ⓘ	sdadmin ✓
Password * ⓘ	•••••••••••• ✓
Confirm password * ⓘ	•••••••••••• ✓

Post update custom configuration

Provide location of an ARM template (inline deployment script, desired state configuration, custom script extension) for post update custom configuration on your session hosts. Provisioning azure resources in the template is not supported. Learn more

ARM template file URL ⓘ	
ARM template parameter file URL ⓘ	

Figure 3-50. *Enter the Virtual Machine details, part 2*

7. On the Workspace tab, select Yes for Register Desktop App Group and choose an existing group or create a new one. Click Next when finished. See Figure 3-51.

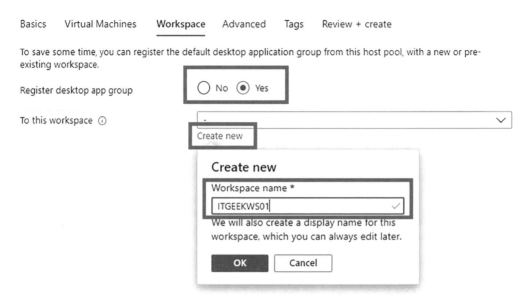

Figure 3-51. *Create a workspace*

8. On the Advanced tab, tick the box if you want to enable diagnostics settings. In this example, we are going to leave it blank. See Figure 3-52. Click Next.

Figure 3-52. *Advanced tab*

9. On the Tags tab, enter any relevant tags you want to add and click Next.

10. Choose Review & Create. Once the validation has passed, choose Create.

This last section discussed hostpools and completed a lab exercise to configure a hostpool in the Azure Portal. In the next exercise, you configure a hostpool via PowerShell.

Creating a Hostpool by Utilizing PowerShell

Before you can start this exercise, ensure you have installed the relevant PowerShell module and logged into Azure via PowerShell. Full instructions can be found at `https://docs.microsoft.com/en-us/azure/virtual-desktop/powershell-module`.

1. To start, run the cmdlet shown in Figure 3-53, which will create the hostpool, workspace, and desktop app group.

```
PS C:\WINDOWS\system32> New-AzWvdHostPool -ResourceGroupName ITGEEKRG01 -Name ITGEEKHP01 -WorkspaceName ITGEEKWS01 -HostPoolType Pooled -LoadBalancerType Bread
thFirst -Location "UK South" -DesktopAppGroupName ITGEEKAppGroup
```

Figure 3-53. *PowerShell cmdlet to create a hostpool, workspace, and desktop app group*

2. Create a registration token to authorize a session host to join the hostpool. Save this to your local PC. The ExpirationTime parameter is used to set how long the registration token is valid. In this example, we set it to three hours. See Figure 3-54.

```
PS C:\WINDOWS\system32> New-AzWvdRegistrationInfo -ResourceGroupName ITGEEKRG01 -HostPoolName ITGEEKHP01 -ExpirationTime $((get-date).ToUniversalTime().AddHour
s(3).ToString('yyyy-MM-ddTHH:mm:ss.fffffffZ'))
```

Figure 3-54. *Create the registration token*

3. Now run a cmdlet to add Azure AD users to the default desktop app group for the hostpool. See Figure 3-55.

```
PS C:\WINDOWS\system32> New-AzRoleAssignment -SignInName "shabaz@iamitgeek.com" -RoleDefinitionName "Desktop Virtualization User" -ResourceName "ITGEEKHP01-DAG
" -ResourceGroupName ITGEEKRG01 -ResourceType 'Microsoft.DesktopVirtualization/applicationGroups'
```

Figure 3-55. *Add an Azure AD user to the default desktop app group*

At this stage the hostpool is created and you can add virtual machines via the Azure Portal.

Assigning the Desktop Application to Users

In the next lab exercise, you will assign a desktop application to the users.

1. In the Azure Virtual Desktop service page, navigate to Application Groups and click the application group you created earlier in this chapter. See Figure 3-56.

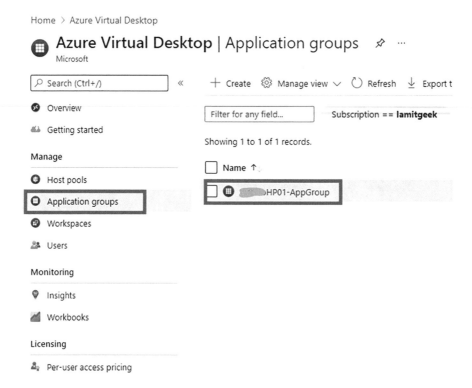

Figure 3-56. *Navigate to Application Groups*

2. Choose Access Control (IAM) ➤ Add ➤ Add Role Assignment, as
    shown in Figure 3-57.

Figure 3-57. *Add Role assignment*

3.   Choose the following values and click Save (see Figure 3-58):

- **Role:** Desktop Virtualization User

- **Assign Access To:** User, group, or service principal

- **Select:** Type the name of a non-admin user account

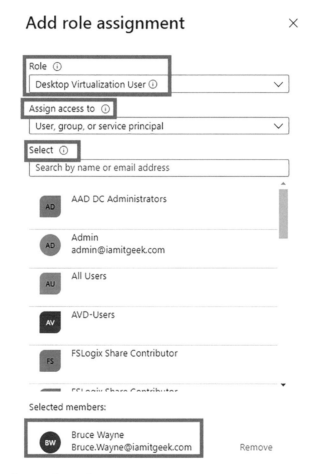

Figure 3-58. *Configure the role assignment*

In this section, you learned how to assign the desktop application to users. In the next section, you will complete a short lab exercise to assign users to the application group.

Assigning Users to the Application Group

1. In the Azure Virtual Desktop Portal, navigate to Application Groups. Choose the application group you created earlier, and then choose Assignments. See Figure 3-59.

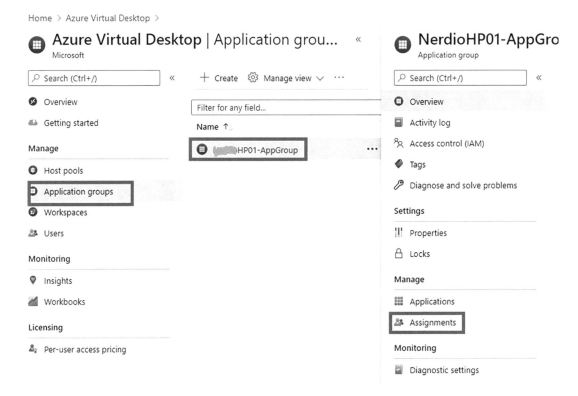

Figure 3-59. *Navigate to Application Group, Assignments*

2. Click Add and search for the user you want to allow access to this application group. Click Select. See Figure 3-60.

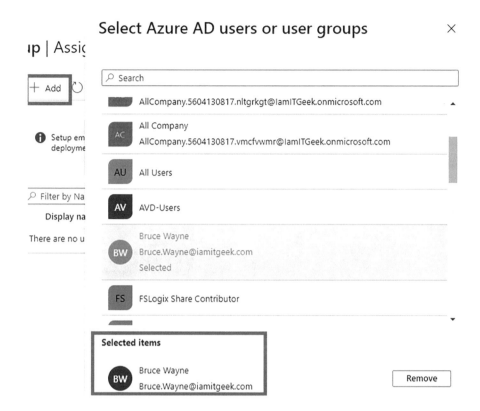

Figure 3-60. *Select the user to grant them access to the application group*

In this next section, we take a look at the various settings that you can manage via the Azure Virtual Desktop Portal and via the Azure Admin Portal.

Managing Hostpool Settings

You can manage several settings for the hostpools via the Admin Portal, including the RDP properties. The RDP properties consist of the following configurable settings:

- Connection information

- Session behavior

- Device redirection

- Display settings

- Advanced options

To configure RDP properties, navigate to Hostpools. Click the hostpool you want to manage and then choose RDP Properties. See Figure 3-61.

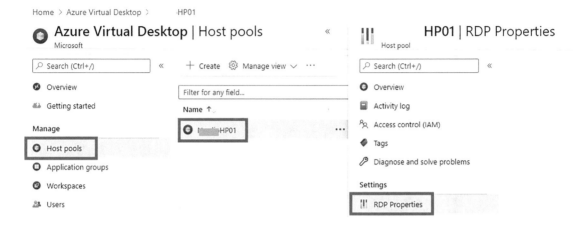

Figure 3-61. *Navigate to RDP properties for the hostpool*

Connection Information

The following settings can be configured from the Connection Information tab (see Figure 3-62):

- **Credential Security Support:** Determines whether Remote Desktop will use CredSSP for authentication if it's available.

- **Alternate Shell:** Specifies a program to be started automatically when you connect to a remote computer. The value should be a valid path to an executable file. This setting only works when connecting to servers.

- **KDC Proxy Name:** (Optional) Enter the fully qualified domain name (FQDN) of the desired KDC proxy.

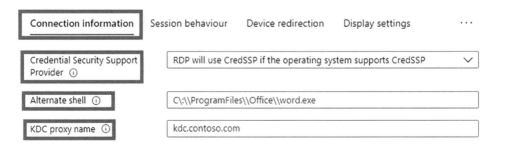

Figure 3-62. *Configure hostpool connection information*

Session Behavior

- **Reconnection:** Determines whether the client computer will automatically try to reconnect to the remote computer if the connection is dropped.

- **Bandwidth Auto Detect:** Determines whether to use automatic network bandwidth detection or not. Requires the option bandwidthautodetect to be set and correlates with connection type 7.

- **Network Auto Detect:** Enables the option for automatic detection of the network type. Used in conjunction with networkautodetect.

- **Compression:** Determines whether the connection should use bulk compression.

- **Video Playback:** Determines whether RDC will use RDP efficient multimedia streaming for video playback. See Figure 3-63.

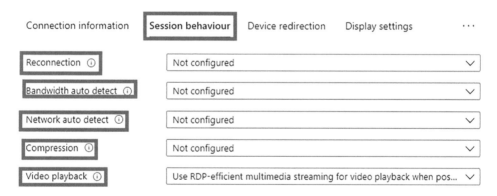

Figure 3-63. *Configure session behavior for the hostpool*

Device Redirection

Audio and Video

- **Microphone:** Determines how sounds captured (recorded) on the local computer are handled when you are connected to the remote computer.

- **Redirected Video Encoding:** Enables or disables encoding of redirected video.

- **Encoded Video Quality:** Controls the quality of encoded video.

- **Audio Output Location:** Determines how sounds captured (recorded) on the local computer are handled when you are connected to the remote computer.

Local Devices and Resources

- **Camera Redirection:** Configures which cameras to redirect. This setting uses a semicolon-delimited list of KSCATEGORY_VIDEO_CAMERA interfaces of cameras enabled for redirection.

- **MTP and PTP Device Redirection:** MTP and PTP device redirection.

- **Drive/Storage Redirection:** Determines which local disk drives on the client computer will be redirected and available in the remote session.

- **Clipboard Redirection:** Determines whether the clipboard on the client computer will be redirected and available in the remote session and vice versa.

- **COM Ports Redirection:** Determines whether the COM (serial) ports on the client computer will be redirected and available in the remote session.

- **Print Redirection:** Determines whether the printer configured on the client computer will be redirected and available on the remote session.

- **Smart Card Redirection:** Determines whether the smart card devices on the client computer will be redirected and available on the remote session.

- **USB Device Redirection:** Determines which supported RemoteFX USB devices on the client computer will be redirected and available in the remote session when you connect to a remote session that supports RemoteFX USB redirection. See Figure 3-64.

| Connection information | Session behaviour | **Device redirection** | Display settings | · · · |

Audio and video

Microphone redirection ⓘ	Not configured ⌄
Redirect video encoding ⓘ	Not configured ⌄
Encoded video quality ⓘ	Not configured ⌄
Audio output location ⓘ	Play sounds on the local computer ⌄

Local devices and resources

Camera redirection ⓘ	Not configured ⌄
MTP and PTP device redirection ⓘ	Redirect portable media players based on the Media Transfer... ⌄
Drive/storage redirection ⓘ	Redirect all disk drives, including ones that are connected later ⌄
Clipboard redirection ⓘ	Clipboard on local computer is available in remote session ⌄
COM ports redirection ⓘ	COM ports on the local computer are available in the remote... ⌄
Printer redirection ⓘ	The printers on the local computer are available in the remot... ⌄
Smart card redirection ⓘ	The smart card device on the local computer is available in t... ⌄
USB device redirection ⓘ	Redirect all USB devices that are not already redirected by an... ⌄

Figure 3-64. *Device redirection settings for hostpools*

Display Settings

- **Multiple Displays:** Determines whether the session should use true multiple monitor support when connecting to the remote session.

- **Selected Monitors:** Specifies which local displays to use from the remote session. The selected displays must be contiguous. Requires use of multimon to be set to 1.

- **Maximize to Current Displays:** Determines which display the remote session goes full screen on when maximizing. Requires the use of multimon to be set to 1.

- **Multi to Single Display Switch:** Determines whether a multi-display remote session automatically switches to single display when exiting full screen. Requires the use of multimon to be set to 1.

- **Screen Mode:** Determines whether the remote session window appears full screen when you connect to the remote computer.

- **Smart Sizing:** Determines whether the client computer should scale the content on the remote computer to fit the window size of the client computer when the window is resized.

- **Dynamic Resolution:** Determines whether the resolution of the remote session is automatically updated when the local window is resized.

- **Desktop Size:** Specifies predefined dimensions of the remote session desktop.

- **Desktop Height (Pixels):** The height (in pixels) of the remote session desktop.

- **Desktop Width (Pixels):** The width (in pixels) of the remote session desktop.

- **Desktop Scale Factor:** Specifies the scale factor of the remote session to make the content appear larger. See Figure 3-65.

Connection information	Session behaviour	Device redirection	**Display settings**	...

Multiple displays ⓘ	Enable multiple display support	⌄
Selected monitors ⓘ	Not configured	⌄
Maximize to current displays ⓘ	Not configured	⌄
Multi to single display switch ⓘ	Not configured	⌄
Screen mode ⓘ	Not configured	⌄
Smart sizing ⓘ	Not configured	⌄
Dynamic resolution ⓘ	Not configured	⌄
Desktop size ⓘ	Not configured	⌄
Desktop height (pixels) ⓘ	0	
Desktop width (pixels) ⓘ	0	
Desktop scale factor ⓘ	Not configured	⌄

Figure 3-65. *Configure display settings for the hostpool*

To access the Advanced settings, you need to click the ... button to right of the window and select Advanced, as shown in Figure 3-66.

Connection information	Session behaviour	Device redirection	Display settings	...

		Connection information
Credential Security Support Provider ⓘ	RDP will use CredSSP if the operating system su	Session behaviour
		Device redirection
Alternate shell ⓘ	C:\\\ProgramFiles\\Office\\word.exe	Display settings
KDC proxy name ⓘ	kdc.contoso.com	Advanced

Figure 3-66. *Navigate to the advanced hostpool settings*

Advanced Settings

- **RDP Properties:** Set custom RDP properties such as multi-monitor experience and audio redirection to deliver an optimal experience for your users. See Figure 3-67.

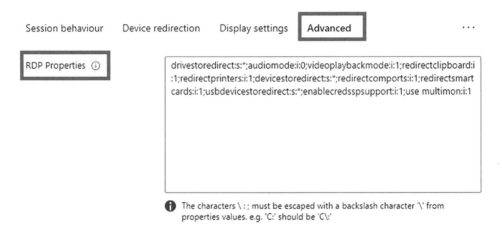

Figure 3-67. *Configure RDP properties for the hostpool*

In this section you looked at creating and configuring hostpools and session hosts, which included several lab exercises in the Azure Portal and PowerShell. The next section takes a closer look at creating and configuring session host images.

Creating and Configuring Session Host Images

This section explains how to create and configure host custom images for your session hosts. We walk through the steps you need to follow to prepare a master virtual hard disk (VHD) image, which can then be uploaded to Azure.

Creating a Gold Image

You can create a golden image from Azure or, if you have specific customizations that need to be implemented on-premises, you can download an image from Azure, customize it, and then upload it back to the image gallery.

Create a Virtual Machine

As mentioned earlier in this chapter, Windows 10 Multi-Session OS is only available from the Azure gallery. There are two options for customizing the image to your requirements:

- *Option 1:* Provision a virtual machine in the Azure Portal. You can follow the steps in the following link to complete this task: `https:// docs.microsoft.com/en-us/azure/virtual-machines/windows/ create-vm-generalized-managed`.

- *Option 2:* Create an image on-premises by downloading the OS image from the Azure gallery, deploying it to Hyper-V, and customizing it as per your requirements. The following lab exercise covers this option.

On-Premises Image Creation

Before you can download the image from Azure, you need to run a Sysprep to generalize the OS.

1. First you need to ensure you have provisioned a VM in Azure with the correct Windows 10 Multi-Session OS.

2. Connect to the virtual machine using Bastion or RDP (Remote Desktop).

3. On the virtual machine, open an elevated command prompt as an administrator.

4. Run the `cd %windir%\system32\sysprep` command to change the directory and run Sysprep.exe.

5. Select Enter System Out-of-Box Experience (OOBE) in the dialog box that opens and ensure you tick the Generalize option.

6. Select Shutdown in the shutdown options and then click OK.

7. Once the VM has shut down, you need go to the Azure Portal and stop the VM.

You have an alternative option of taking a snapshot of the VM disk and then downloading and importing it into Hyper-V.

Generate URL for Downloading

Now that you have generalized the Windows 10 Multi-Session OS in Azure, you need to
download it locally to your on-premises environment.

1. In the Azure Portal, on the VM page, click Disks in the left pane.
   See Figure 3-68.

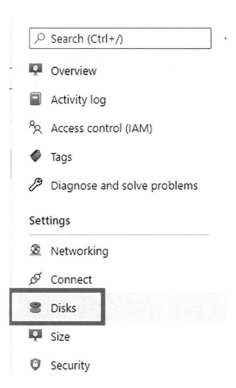

Figure 3-68. *Navigate to the VM's disks*

2. Choose the OS disk.

3. On the Disks page, choose Disk Export from the left menu pane, as
   shown in Figure 3-69.

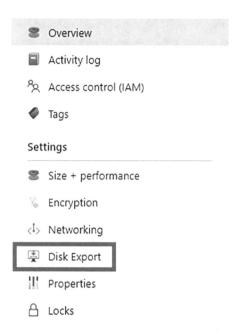

Figure 3-69. *Disk Export menu*

4. Note that the default URL Expire In time is set to 3600 seconds
    (1 hour). Depending on how large the disk is, you might want to
    increase this. 36000 (10 hours) will cover most scenarios. Click
    Generate URL once you set the expiration time; see Figure 3-70.

Figure 3-70. *Generate URL for download*

5. Once the URL has been generated, click the Download the VHD
    File link under the URL. See Figure 3-71.

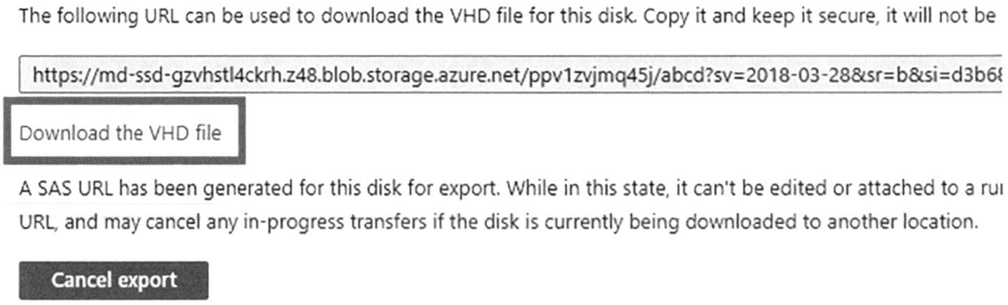

The following URL can be used to download the VHD file for this disk. Copy it and keep it secure, it will not be

https://md-ssd-gzvhstl4ckrh.z48.blob.storage.azure.net/ppv1zvjmq45j/abcd?sv=2018-03-28&sr=b&si=d3b6£

Download the VHD file

A SAS URL has been generated for this disk for export. While in this state, it can't be edited or attached to a ru
URL, and may cancel any in-progress transfers if the disk is currently being downloaded to another location.

Cancel export

Figure 3-71. *Download the VHD disk from the Azure Portal*

Local Image Creation

When the image is fully downloaded to your local infrastructure, you can open Hyper-V to create a new VM using the VHD you downloaded. The following is a simple walk-though of how you can do this. For a more in-depth guide, refer to `https://docs.microsoft.com/en-us/windows-server/virtualization/hyper-v/get-started/create-a-virtual-machine-in-hyper-v/`.

1. In Hyper-V Manager, open the New Virtual Machine wizard.

2. Choose Generation 1 on the Specify Generation page.

3. Disable checkpoints under Checkpoint Type.

You created the virtual machine from an existing VHD, which you downloaded from Azure. Hyper-V will create the disk as a dynamic disk by default, so you need to change this to a fixed disk by editing the disk.

Once the VM is in Hyper-V, you can boot it up and configure the customizations you require. This may include registry entries, software installs, and other OS customizations. Once this exercise is finished, you need to prepare the Windows VHD or VHDX to upload to Azure. You can find detailed instructions at `https://docs.microsoft.com/en-us/azure/virtual-machines/windows/prepare-for-upload-vhd-image`.

After the customized image is ready and uploaded to Azure, you need to complete steps to redo the Sysprep in Azure and complete the image capture steps, which will save it into the image gallery. The following exercise outlines how to complete these steps.

Image Capture

The following steps walk through how to capture an image of a virtual machine in Azure.

1. Navigate to the virtual machine you want to capture in the Azure Portal.

2. In the Virtual Machine Overview tab, ensure that the status is showing as Stopped (Deallocated). If this is not the case, click Stop from the top menu bar. See Figure 3-72.

Figure 3-72. *Ensure VM is in stop state*

3. Once the VM is in a stopped state, click the Capture button at the top of the menu. This will open the Create an Image window (see Figures 3-73 and 3-74).

4. Complete the Basics tab with all the relevant information. In this example, we use the following values:

   - **Subscription:** You trial Azure subscription.

   - **Resource Group:** Resource group you created in Chapter 2.

   - Share image to Shared image gallery: Choose Yes.

   - **Target Image Gallery:** Click Create New and enter the name of your new gallery.

- **Operating System State:** Ensure Generalized is selected.

- **Target Image Definition:** This is the parent definition for this version of the image. Click Create New. On the Create an Image Definition pane on the right side, enter a relevant name, then click OK.

- **Version Number:** Enter the value of 0.0.1 as this is the first version. For all subsequent versions you will go up one number. For example, 0.0.2, 0.0.3, and so on. See Figures 3-73 and 3-74.

Create an image   ⋯

Basics   Tags   Review + create

Create an image from this virtual machine that can be used to deploy additional virtual machines and virtual machine scale sets. With a shared image, you can easily replicate the image to Azure regions around the world and manage versions of the image. Certain information from the virtual machine will be carried forward to the image including OS type, VM generation, plan, and publishing details. Learn more ☐

Project details

Subscription   Iamitgeek

└──── Resource group *   ITGEEKRG01

Instance details

Region   (Europe) UK South

Share image to Shared image gallery ⓘ   ◉ Yes, share it to a gallery as an image version.
                                                   ○ No, capture only a managed image.

Automatically delete this virtual machine   ☐
after creating the image ⓘ

Gallery details

Target image gallery * ⓘ   (new) ITGEEKGA01
                                                   Create new

Operating system state ⓘ   ◉ Generalized: VMs created from this image require hostname, admin user, and
                                                   other VM related setup to be completed on first boot

                                                   ○ Specialized: VMs created from this image are completely configured and do
                                                   not require parameters such as hostname and admin user/password

Figure 3-73. Create an Image, part 1

Target image definition * ⓘ — (new) itgeekdef01 ⌄
Create new

Version details

Version number * ⓘ — 0.0.1 ✓

Exclude from latest ⓘ — ☐

End of life date ⓘ — MM/DD/YYYY 📅

Replication

An image version can be replicated to different regions depending on what makes sense for your organization. One example is to always replicate the latest image in multiple regions while all older versions are only available in 1 region. This can help save on storage costs for image versions.

Default replica count * ⓘ — 1

Target regions	Target region replica count	Storage account type	
(Europe) UK South ⌄	1	Standard HDD LRS ⌄	🗑
⌄	1	Standard HDD LRS ⌄	

Figure 3-74. *Create an Image, PART 2*

The process of updating the image is similar to creating the initial image; however as mentioned, you change the version number to ensure it is the latest version in the image gallery.

Add New Session Hosts to an Existing Hostpool

When your image creation is done and you have captured the latest version, you are ready to replace the existing session hosts in your hostpool with the latest image. The following steps outline how to do this.

1. Navigate to the session hosts in the Azure Virtual Desktop Service Portal.

2. Select the existing virtual machines and click Turn Drain Mode On in the top menu. This will stop any new logins to the session hosts. Note that in a production environment you will need to schedule an outage for this.

3. Click + Add. If you see the warning shown in Figure 3-75, you need to click this and create a registration key.

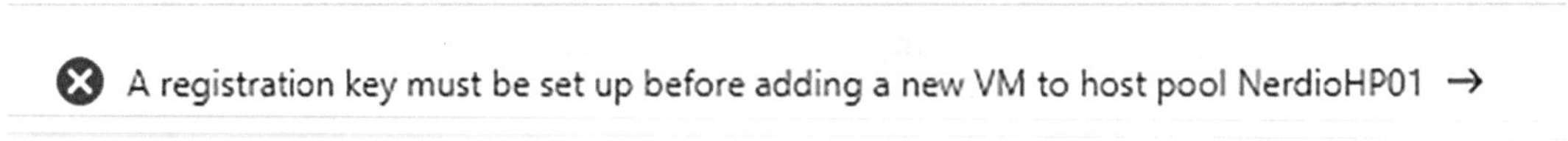

❌ A registration key must be set up before adding a new VM to host pool NerdioHP01 →

Figure 3-75. *Registration key warning*

4. You should now be on the Add Virtual Machines to a Host Pool page after the registration key is generated (if required). The Basics tab will be fully prepopulated and grayed out. Click Next.

5. On the Virtual Machines tab, complete all the values as you did in the lab exercise earlier in this chapter where you created your first hostpool. The only difference is that under Image. Choose See all images ➤ My Items. Then select the custom captured image you created earlier.

6. You can leave the Advanced and Tags tabs as their defaults for the purposes of this lab exercise.

Once you have validated and clicked Create, this will deploy the new version of the VMs to your hostpool and users can then start to log in again. Once all the sessions from the old session hosts are cleared, you can remove them from your hostpool.

This section discussed how to create a new image from the Azure Portal, customize an image locally, and capture and update an image in Azure.

Knowledge Check

The following questions are aimed at testing your understanding of the information in this chapter. It is recommended to complete all the sections and labs in this chapter before attempting these questions.

Check Your Knowledge

1. Your organization has a set of programmers that need virtual desktops that they can manage. What type of hostpool would be the best fit for this use case?

   - Personal

   - Pooled

   - Local

2. What OS image should you use with a pooled hostpool?

   - Windows 10 Pro

   - Windows 10 Enterprise Multi-Session

   - An image that can support multi-session workloads

3. How do you give users access to applications and a remote desktop?

   - This is not possible. Users can only belong to a single group type.

   - Assign the users to the RemoteApp and Desktop Application groups.

   - Create a new application group for RemoteApp and assign it to Azure AD users/groups.

4. What two IAM services can you integrate with an Azure Storage account?

   - Azure AD

   - Active Directory Domain Services

   - Azure AD DS

5. What step do you need to complete to create a new image in the image gallery?

   - Capture the Windows VM image

   - Snapshot the OS disk

   - Sysprep the Windows OS

Summary

This chapter looked at how to implement and manage networking for Azure Virtual Desktop, how to implement and manage storage for Azure Virtual Desktop, how to create and configure hostpools and session hosts, and how to create and manage session host images. You also completed several lab exercises, including provisioning a site-to-site VPN between Azure and your on-premises location, creating an Azure File share and integrating your storage account with Active Directory, provisioning a session host, and creating a new image from Azure and locally.

Chapter 4 takes a deep dive into managing access and security in Azure Virtual Desktop, including managing access to Azure Virtual Desktop and managing security for Azure Virtual Desktop.

CHAPTER 4

Manage Access and Security to Azure Virtual Desktop

The previous chapter took a deeper look into implementing and managing an Azure Virtual Desktop Architecture, including implementing and managing networking for Azure Virtual Desktop, implementing and managing storage for Azure Virtual Desktop, creating and configuring hostpools and sessions hosts, and creating and managing session host images.

This chapter covers the following main topics:

- Managing access to Azure Virtual Desktop

- Managing security to Azure Virtual Desktop

- Knowledge check

Technical Requirements

To complete the exercises in this book, you need to have access to a Microsoft 365 tenant. This can be attained by signing up for a trial subscription. Additionally, Azure Virtual Desktop services require one of the following licenses:

- Microsoft 365 Business Premium

- Microsoft 365 E5/E3

- Microsoft 365 A3/A5/Student Benefits

- Microsoft 365 F3

127

© Shabaz Darr 2022
S. Darr, *Azure Virtual Desktop Specialist*, https://doi.org/10.1007/978-1-4842-7987-8_4

- Windows 10 Enterprise E3/E5

- Windows 10 Education A3/A5

- Windows 10 VDA per user

Managing Access to Azure Virtual Desktop

Microsoft cloud services that are hosted in Azure utilize role-based access control (RBAC), including Azure Virtual Desktop. RBAC allows you to give access to users depending on their role.

Azure has its standard built-in roles such as Owner, Contributor, and Reader; however, there are additional roles that are more specific to Azure Virtual Desktop. This section discusses these roles and the level of access they grant a user who is assigned the specific role.

Built-in Roles for Azure Virtual Desktop

The following built-in RBAC roles are specific to Azure Virtual Desktop and have different levels of access.

- **Desktop Virtualization Contributor**: This role allows you to handle and manage all areas of your Azure Virtual Desktop deployment. If you want to publish app groups to users or groups, you also need to assign the User Access Administrator with this role. This role will not enable you to access any of the compute resources. The following list shows the exact permissions that this role will grant you:

  - Microsoft.DesktopVirtualization/*

  - Microsft.Resources/Subscriptions/resourceGroups/read

  - Microsft.Resources/deployments/*

  - Microsoft.Authorizations/*/read

  - Microsoft.Insights/alertRules/*

  - Microsoft.Support/*

- **Desktop Virtualization Reader:** If you assign this role to a member of the admin team, they will be able to view everything in the Azure Virtual Desktop deployment; however, they will not be able to make any changes. The following list shows the exact permissions that this role will grant you:

    - Microsoft.DesktopVirtualization/*/read

    - Microsoft.Resources/Subscriptions/resourceGroups/read

    - Microsoft.Resources/deployments/read

    - Microsoft.Authorizations/*/read

    - Microsoft.Insights/alertRules/*

    - Microsoft.Support/*

- **Desktop Virtualization Hostpool Contributor:** This role will enable you to manage all areas of the hostpool as well as access all the resources. If you want to create virtual machines as part of this, you will additionally need the Virtual Machine Role Contributor role. If you want to create hostpools using the Azure Admin Portal, you need to assign the AppGroup and Workspace contributor roles, or the Desktop Virtualization Contributor role. The following list shows the permissions that this role will enable for you:

    - Microsoft.DesktopVirtualization/Hostpools/*

    - Microsoft.Resources/subscriptions/resourceGroups/read

    - Microsoft.Resources/deployments/*

    - Microsoft.Authorization/*/read

    - Microsoft.Insights/alertRules/*

    - Microsoft.Support/*

- **Desktop Virtualization Hostpool Reader:** This is a read-only role that will not allow the admin user to make any amendment; however it does allow them to view the entire hostpool. The following list shows the permissions that this role will enable for you:

- Microsoft.DesktopVirtulization/Hostpools/*/read

- Microsoft.Resources/subscriptions/resourceGroups/read

- Microsoft.Resources/Deployments/read

- Microsoft.Authorization/*/read

- Microsoft.Insights/alertRules/*

- Microsoft.Support/*

- **Desktop Virtualization Application Group Contributor:** If you assign this role to an administrator, it will enable them to manage all areas of app groups. You need to assign the User Access Administrator role if you want the same user to be able to publish app groups. The following list shows the permissions that this role will enable for you:

  - Microsoft.DesktopVirtualization/applicationgroups/*

  - Microsoft.DesktopVirtualization/hostpools/read

  - Microsoft.DesktopVirtualization/hostpools/sessionhosts/read

  - Microsoft.Resources/subscriptions/resourceGroups/read

  - Microsoft.Resources/deployments/*

  - Microsoft.Authorization/*/read

  - Microsoft.Insights/alertRules/*

  - Microsoft.Support/*

- **Desktop Virtualization Application Group Reader:** Assigning this role to an administrator will allow them to read all areas within an app group; however they cannot make changes. The following list shows the permissions that this role will enable for you:

  - Microsoft.DesktopVirtualization/applicationgroups/*/read

  - Microsoft.DesktopVirtualization/applicationgroups/read

  - Microsoft.DesktopVirtualization/hostpools/read

  - Microsoft.DesktopVirtualization/hostpools/sessionhosts/read

- Microsoft.Resources/subscriptions/resourceGroups/read

- Microsoft.Resources/deployments/read

- Microsoft.Authorization/*/read

- Microsoft.Insights/alertRules/*

- Microsoft.Support/*

- **Desktop Virtualization Workspace Contributor:** This role will enable you to fully access and manage all areas of the workspace. You will need to assign the Application Group Reader role to the user if they require information on the application group. The following list shows the permissions that this role will enable for you:

  - Microsoft.DesktopVirtualization/workspaces/*

  - Microsoft.DesktopVirtualization/applicationgroups/read

  - Microsoft.Resources/subscriptions/resourceGroups/read

  - Microsoft.Resources/deployments/*

  - Microsoft.Authorization/*/read

  - Microsoft.Insights/alertRules/*

  - Microsoft.Support/*

- **Desktop Virtualization Workspace Reader:** This role will enable you to read/view all aspects of the workspace; however you cannot modify any resources. The following list shows the permissions that this role will enable for you:

  - Microsoft.DesktopVirtualization/workspaces/read

  - Microsoft.DesktopVirtualization/applicationgroups/read

  - Microsoft.Resources/subscriptions/resourceGroups/read

  - Microsoft.Resources/deployments/read

  - Microsoft.Authorization/*/read

  - Microsoft.Insights/alertRules/*

  - Microsoft.Support/*

- **Desktop Virtualization User Session Operator:** This role enables you to send messages, disconnect sessions, and log users off from the Azure Virtual Desktop Portal. This role does not give you permission to manage session home management, for example deleting a session host from the hostpool and enabling/disabling drain mode. The user who is assigned this role can view assignments, but they will not be able to amend admins. It is recommended to assign this role to a hostpool. The following list shows the permissions that this role will enable for you:

  - Microsoft.DesktopVirtualization/hostpools/read

  - Microsoft.DesktopVirtualization/hostpools/sessionhosts/read

  - Microsoft.DesktopVirtualization/hostpools/sessionhosts/usersessions/*

  - Microsoft.Resources/subscriptions/resourceGroups/read

  - Microsoft.Resources/deployments/read

  - Microsoft.Authorization/*/read

  - Microsoft.Insights/alertRules/*

  - Microsoft.Support/*

- **Desktop Virtualization Session Host Operator:** This role will enable you to see and delete session hosts and can enable/disable drain mode. Users need to have writer permissions to hostpool objects if they want to be able to add session hosts. You can add sessions hosts if you are assigned the Virtual Machine Contributor role (as long as the registration token is still valid). The following list shows the permissions that this role will enable for you:

  - Microsoft.DesktopVirtualization/hostpools/read

  - Microsoft.DesktopVirtualization/hostpools/sessionhosts/*

  - Microsoft.Resources/subscriptions/resourceGroups/read

  - Microsoft.Resources/deployments/read

  - Microsoft.Authorization/*/read

- Microsoft.Insights/alertRules/*

- Microsoft.Support/*

This section discussed RBAC roles that are specific to Azure Virtual Desktop. The next section is a lab exercise to assign a role to an Azure Virtual Desktop service via the Azure Portal and PowerShell.

Assigning Role-Based Assignment to Azure Virtual Desktop

The following two lab exercises walk you through how to assign roles via the Azure Portal and via PowerShell.

Assign Role-Based Assignment via Admin Center

The following lab walks through the steps to assign a role to an Azure Virtual Desktop resource.

1. Open a web browser and go to the Azure Portal via `https://portal.azure.com`.

2. Navigate to the Azure Virtual Desktop platform by typing it in the search box and selecting it from the list that appears. See Figure 4-1.

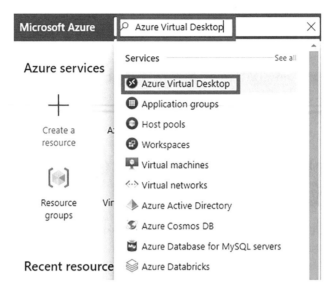

Figure 4-1. *Navigate to the Azure Virtual Desktop service in the portal*

3. In this example, we are going to assign a role to the hostpool, so we need to navigate to the hostpool section. If you want to assign a specific role to another resource (application groups or workspaces, for example), you need to navigate to those sections.

4. In the Hostpool menu, select Access Control (IAM). See Figure 4-2.

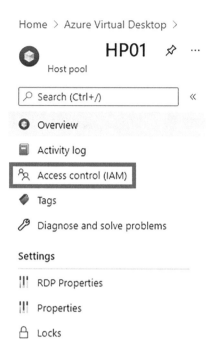

Figure 4-2. *Navigate to Access Control (IAM) section of Azure Virtual Desktop*

5. On the Access Control page, click the +Add option, as shown in
    Figure 4-3.

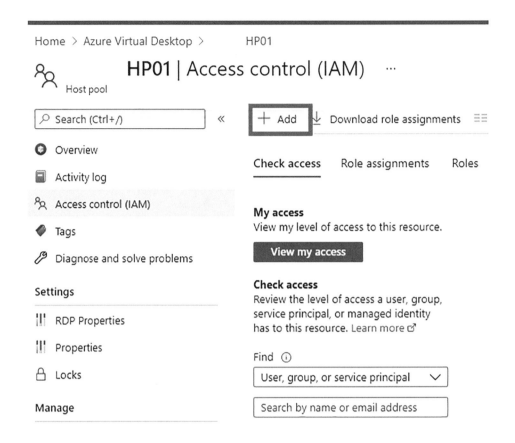

Figure 4-3. *Click Add*

6. Select Add Role Assignment, as shown in Figure 4-4.

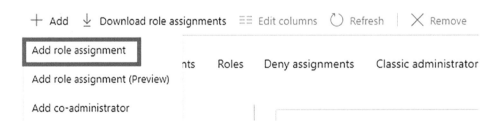

Figure 4-4. *Add Role Assignment*

7. In the Add Role Assignment section, in the Role text field, type
desktop virtualization hostpool to show all the hostpool-related
roles. See Figure 4-5.

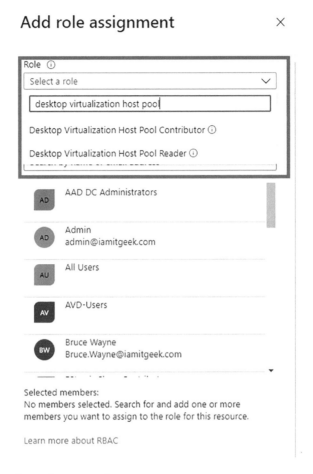

Figure 4-5. *Select the relevant role*

8. In this example, you assign the Desktop Virtualization Hostpool Contributor to an administrator account. Click Save.

Assign Role-Based Assignment via PowerShell

In this exercise, you learn how to assign a role via PowerShell:

1. Log in to Azure via PowerShell. Follow the instructions at `https://docs.microsoft.com/en-us/powershell/azure/ authenticate-azureps?view=azps-6.4.0`.

2. Ensure you understand the specific role you want to grant access
    to. You can list the roles and get specific role IDs by using the
    cmdlet shown in Figure 4-6.

```
PS C:\WINDOWS\system32> Get-AzRoleDefinition | FT Name, IsCustom, Id
```

Figure 4-6. *Get a list of Azure roles and document the specific one you want to grant access to*

3. In this example, we will pick the Desktop Virtualization
    Application Group Reader role to a user, which is shown in
    Figure 4-7.

```
Desktop Virtualization Application Group Reader          False aebf23d0-b568-4e86-b8f9-fe83a2c6ab55
```

Figure 4-7. *Desktop Virtualization Application Group Reader Role in PowerShell*

4. There are different levels of scope you can assign permissions to,
    including:

    - **Resource scope:** You need the resource ID for this, which can be
      found in the properties of the resource in the Azure Portal.

    - **Resource group scope:** You need the name of the resource group
      for this, which can be found on the Resource Group page.

    - **Subscription scope:** You need the subscription ID, which can be
      found on the Subscriptions page.

    - **Management group scope:** You need the management group
      name, which can be found on the Management Groups page.

    In this example, we will assign the Desktop Virtualization
    Application Group Reader role to an admin user and specify the
    Application Group Resource.

5. Complete the cmdlet in Figure 4-8 to assign the Desktop
    Virtualization Application Group Reader to an admin user, scoped
    to the Application Group resource.

```
PS C:\WINDOWS\system32> New-AzRoleAssignment -SignInName shabaz@iamitgeek.com `
>> -RoleDefinitionName "Desktop Virtualization Application Group Reader" `
>> -ResourceName          -AppGroup `
>> -ResourceType Microsoft.DesktopVirtualization/applicationgroups `
>> -ResourceGroupName ITGEEKRG03
```

Figure 4-8. *New Role Assignment cmdlet*

This section discussed role-based access control (RBAC) and how you can use it to plan and implement roles for Azure Virtual Desktop. You also completed the lab exercises, which walk through how to assign roles to Azure Virtual Desktop via the Azure Center and via PowerShell.

The next section discusses delegated access in Azure Virtual Desktop and explains how you can configure user restrictions by utilizing Azure AD group policies and AD policies with Intune integration.

Delegated Access in Azure Virtual Desktop

When you utilize the delegated access model with Azure Virtual Desktop, it allows you to define the amount of access specific users can have by assigning them a specific role. There are three main components of a role assignment: security principal, role definition, and scope.

The following values are supported for each element when configuring delegated access for Azure Virtual Desktop:

- Security principal
    - Users
    - User groups
    - Service principals
- Role definition
    - Built-in roles
    - Custom roles
- Scope
    - Hostpools
    - App groups
    - Workspaces

In the following labs, we walk through how to add an Azure AD user to an app group via the Azure Portal and via PowerShell.

Add an Azure AD User to an Application Group via Azure Admin Center

1. Log in to the Azure Admin Center at `https://portal.azure.com` and navigate to the Azure Virtual Desktop services page.

2. Navigate to Application Groups, as shown in Figure 4-9.

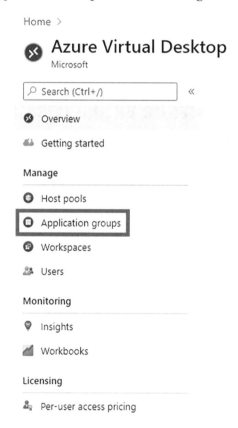

Figure 4-9. *Navigate to Application Groups*

3. Select the relevant application group you want to assign users or groups to, as shown in Figure 4-10.

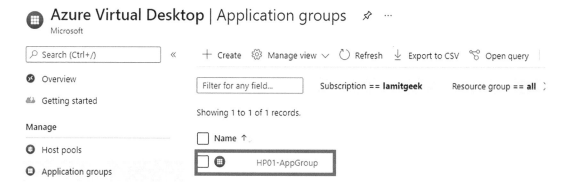

Figure 4-10. *Select the relevant application group*

4. On the Application Group page, navigate to Manage ➤
    Assignments, as shown in Figure 4-11.

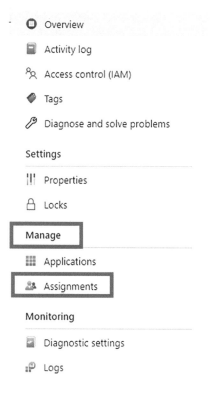

Figure 4-11. *Navigate to Assignments page*

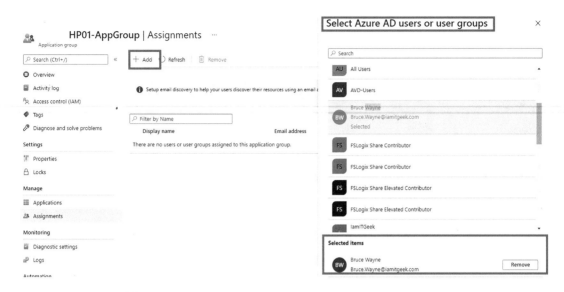

Figure 4-12. *Add a user/group assignment to an application group*

5. Click the +Add button and then select the user or group you want
    to assign permissions to in the application group. Click Select. See
    Figure 4-11.

Add an Azure AD User to an Application Group via PowerShell

1. First you need to set up the PowerShell module on your computer
    for Azure Virtual Desktop. Run the cmdlet shown in Figure 4-13 in
    an elevated PowerShell window to install the relevant module.

```
PS C:\WINDOWS\system32> Install-Module -Name Az.DesktopVirtualization
```

Figure 4-13. *Install Azure Virtual Desktop module for PowerShell*

2. Run the cmdlet shown in Figure 4-14 to connect to Azure via
    PowerShell. You will be prompted to enter your global admin
    credentials.

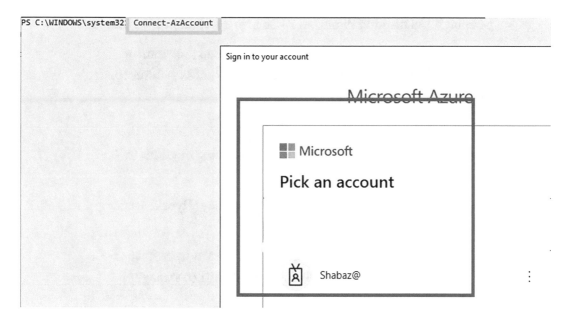

Figure 4-14. *Connect to Azure via PowerShell cmdlet*

3. Run the cmdlet shown in Figure 4-15 to grant user access to the application group.

Figure 4-15. *Configure assignment to an application group via PowerShell*

This section discussed delegated access and completed lab exercises to assign access to an application group via the Azure Portal and PowerShell. The next section discusses how you can configure user restrictions by utilizing Azure AD group policies and AD policies with Intune integration.

Azure Virtual Desktop Integration with Intune

Azure Virtual Desktop is called a DaaS (Desktop as a Service) platform in which you can virtualize applications and Windows Desktops. Integrating this platform with Intune enables you to manage and secure the session hosts by utilizing policies once they are enrolled.

At the present, Intune integration supports the following Azure Virtual Desktop VM scenarios:

- Session hosts running Windows 10 Enterprise, version 1809 (or later)

- Session hosts need to be hybrid Azure AD joined (See more at
  `https://docs.microsoft.com/en-us/azure/active-directory/`
  `devices/hybrid-azuread-join-plan`)

- Personal hostpool registered session hosts

- Intune enrolled. You can use one of the following methods to
  accomplish this:

  - Auto enroll devices by utilizing Group policy (Hybrid Azure
    AD Join)

  - Co-management with Config Manager (see more at `https://`
    `docs.microsoft.com/en-us/mem/configmgr/comanage/`
    `overview`)

  - Azure AD join with user self-enrollment (see more at `https://`
    `docs.microsoft.com/en-us/mem/intune/enrollment/windows-`
    `enrollment-methods#user-self-enrollment-in-intune`)

  - Enable the feature to enroll the VM with Intune in the Azure
    Portal (see more at `https://docs.microsoft.com/en-us/azure/`
    `virtual-desktop/deploy-azure-ad-joined-vm#deploy-azure-`
    `ad-joined-vms`)

This section discussed various topics related to managing access to Azure Virtual Desktop, including built-in roles, assigning RBAC roles, delegating roles, and integration with Intune. The next section discusses how to manage security with Azure Virtual Desktop.

Managing Security on Azure Virtual Desktop

To manage security on your Azure Virtual Desktop, you first need to understand the responsibility model, as it is important to understand that Microsoft takes responsibility for securing specific services.

Table 4-1 outlines the Azure Virtual Desktop specific services that are managed by Microsoft.

Table 4-1. *Azure Virtual Desktop Microsoft Managed Services*

Service	Description
Web Access	Allows users to access the application group resources (desktop or remoteapp) via an HTMLv5-compatible Internet browser.
Gateway	Connects remote user's connection to a gateway, then creates a connection from the virtual machine back to the same gateway.
Broker	Allows load-balancing and facilitates reconnections to the application group resources (desktop and remoteapp).
Diagnostics	Allows event logs of actions on the AVD deployment as success or failure. Useful for troubleshooting
Infrastructure services (Azure)	Networking, storage, and other compute services in Azure are managed by Microsoft.

Table 4-2 outlines the Azure Virtual Desktop-specific components that are managed by the end users/clients.

Table 4-2. *Azure Virtual Desktop Client Managed Services*

Component	Description
End user profile management	Azure Files integration with FSLogix enables a containerized user profile experience.
End user host access	There are two types of load-balancing algorithms—depth and or breadth—which are defined when the hostpool is created.
Virtual machine scaling and sizing	Sizing components for virtual machines, including GPU-enabled VMs.
Policies for scaling	VMs (session hosts) can be load-balanced using scale sets.
Policies for networking	The consumer/client is required to create Network Security Groups (NSGs) that filter network traffic.

Ensuring secure access to the Azure Virtual Desktop environment is an essential part of the deployment, and it will also be important for the exam. Azure Active Directory allows you to configure Conditional Access policies and Multi-Factor Authentication (MFA) integration with the Azure Virtual Desktop platform, which creates an additional layer of security.

This section covered the responsibility model from an Azure Virtual Desktop perspective, which highlights the services that Microsoft manages and the services that the end consumer is required to manage. We will not look at securing Azure Virtual Desktop with Conditional Access Policies.

Configuring a Conditional Access Policy to Enable MFA

In the following lab exercise, we walk through how to configure a Conditional Access policy that will enforce the end user to register to MFA. They must use this whenever they connect to the Azure Virtual Desktop environment.

1. Log in to the Azure Portal at `https://portal.azure.com` with an account that is assigned one of the following roles:

    - Global Administrator

    - Security Administrator

    - Conditional Access Administrator

2. Navigate to Azure Active Directory ➤ Security ➤ Conditional Access, as shown in Figure 4-16.

Figure 4-16. *Navigate to Conditional Access Polices in Azure AD*

3. Click on + New Policy, as shown in Figure 4-17.

Figure 4-17. *Create a new conditional access policy*

4. In the Name field, give the policy an appropriate name.

5. *In* the Assignments - User and Groups field, select the users or groups you want this policy to be applicable to. See Figure 4-18.

Figure 4-18. *Assign permissions to a user or group*

6. Choose Cloud Apps or Actions ➤ Include ➤ Select Apps. At this point you need to search for one of the following Azure Virtual Desktop apps if you are using the Classic version:

- Azure Virtual Desktop (App ID 5a0aa725-4958-4b0c-80a9-34562e23f3b7)

- Azure Virtual Desktop Client (App ID fa4345a4-a730-4230-84a8-7d9651b86739), which will let you set policies on the web client

Otherwise, you can search for the Windows Virtual Desktop app
if you're using the Azure Resource Manager (ARM) version.
See Figure 4-19.

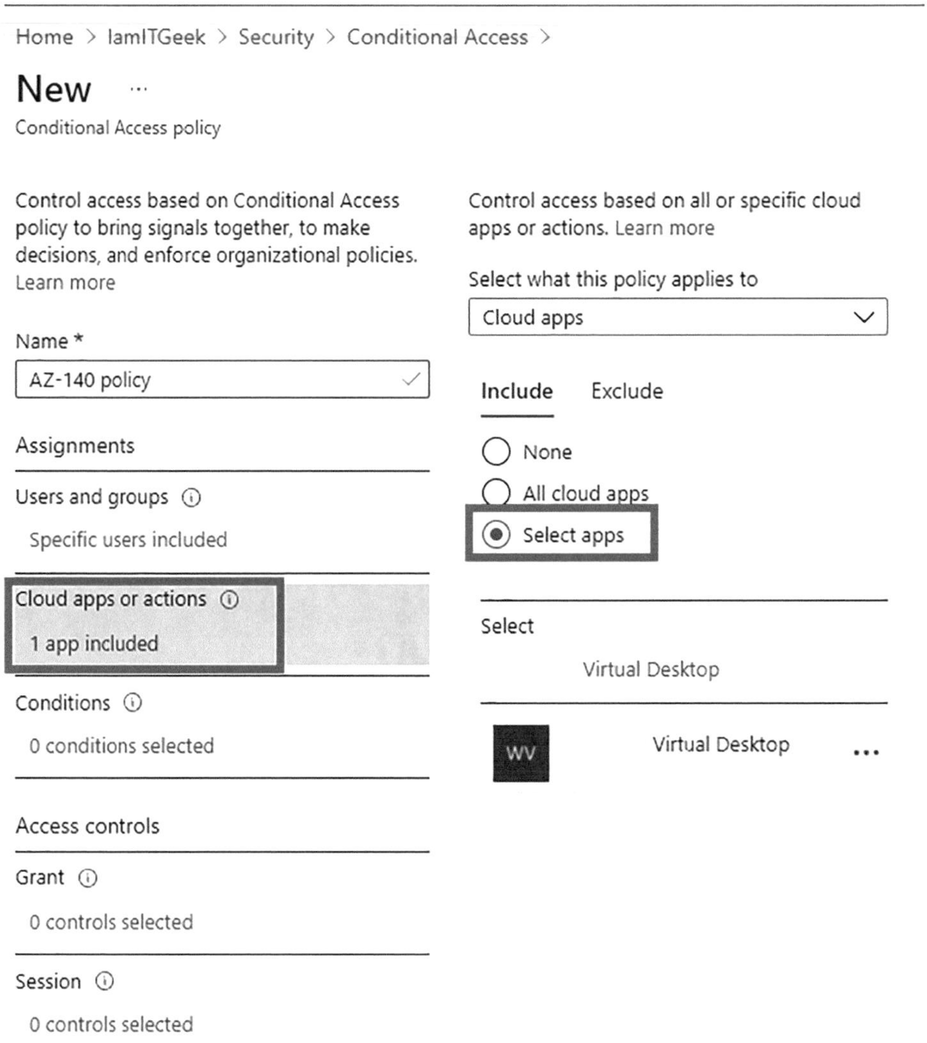

Home > IamITGeek > Security > Conditional Access >

New ...
Conditional Access policy

Control access based on Conditional Access
policy to bring signals together, to make
decisions, and enforce organizational policies.
Learn more

Name *

AZ-140 policy

Assignments

Users and groups ⓘ

  Specific users included

Cloud apps or actions ⓘ

  1 app included

Conditions ⓘ

  0 conditions selected

Access controls

Grant ⓘ

  0 controls selected

Session ⓘ

  0 controls selected

Control access based on all or specific cloud
apps or actions. Learn more

Select what this policy applies to

Cloud apps ⌄

Include   Exclude

◯ None

◯ All cloud apps

◉ Select apps

Select

  Virtual Desktop

  WV   Virtual Desktop   ...

Figure 4-19. *Assign the Azure Virtual Desktop App to this policy*

7. Choose Conditions ➤ Client Apps. Click Yes on Configure
    and then ensure that only Mobile Apps and Desktop Clients is
    selected, as shown in Figure 4-20.

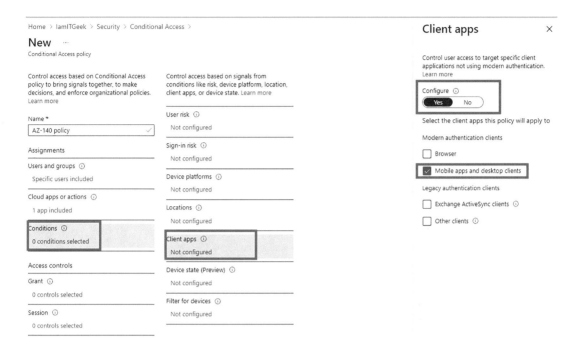

Figure 4-20. *Configure Client App conditions*

8. Under Access Controls, choose Grant Access and ensure you tick
Require Multi-Factor Authentication. See Figure 4-21.

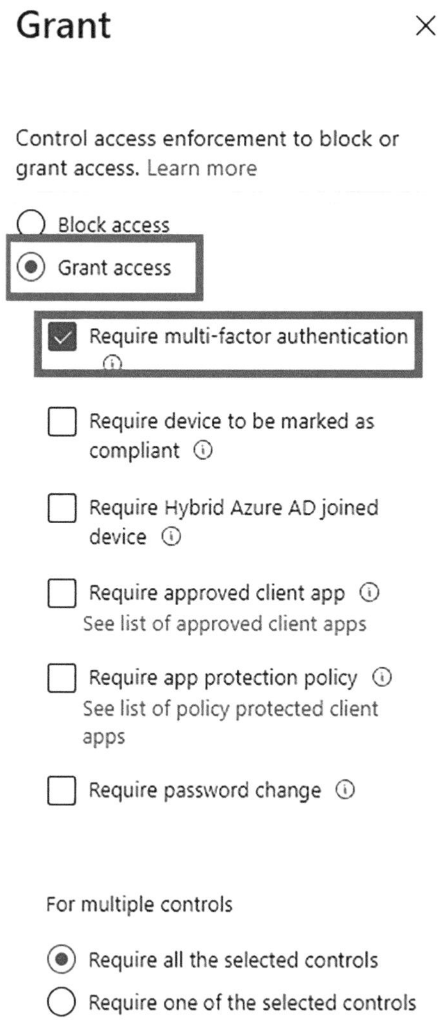

Figure 4-21. *Configure grant access controls*

9. Choose Session under Access Controls and tick the box next to
   Sign-in Frequency. You can then decide how much time you want
   to set between users being promoted for MFA authentication. In
   this example, we set it to five days. See Figure 4-22.

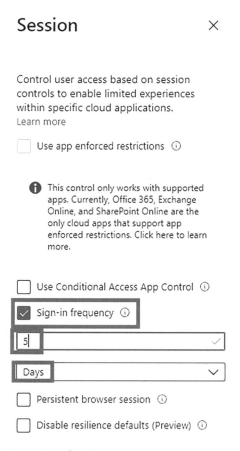

Figure 4-22. *Set the session time limit*

10. Once you have configured the policy, make sure you select On to
    turn the policy on. Then click Create at the bottom of the page; see
    Figure 4-23.

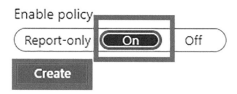

Figure 4-23. *Enable and create the policy*

This section included a lab exercise to enable MFA by configuring a Conditional
Access policy. The next section covers some security best practices for Azure Virtual
Desktop.

Azure Virtual Desktop Security Best Practices

There are multiple security controls that are built into the Azure Virtual Desktop platform. This section discusses what they are and how they integrate into this service.

Multi-Factor Authentication

In the previous section, you completed a lab exercise to configure multi-factor authentication. Making this a requirement for all users who are accessing Azure Virtual Desktop is an essential security best practice.

Configure Conditional Access

Conditional access policies will enable admins to control and manage risk before users can access the platform. It is recommended that you think about who the users are, how they are logging in, and the device users are connecting from before you give them access to the Azure Virtual Desktop platform.

Audit Logs

You can monitor admin activity associated with the Azure Virtual Desktop environment when you enable audit log collections. The following are some of the audit logs you can utilize:

- Key Vault logs (`https://docs.microsoft.com/en-us/azure/key-vault/general/logging`)

- Azure Activity log (`https://docs.microsoft.com/en-us/azure/azure-monitor/essentials/activity-log`)

- Azure Virtual Desktop Diagnostic log (`https://docs.microsoft.com/en-us/azure/virtual-desktop/diagnostics-log-analytics`)

- Azure Active Directory Activity log (`https://docs.microsoft.com/en-us/azure/active-directory/reports-monitoring/concept-activity-logs-azure-monitor`)

- Session Hosts (`https://docs.microsoft.com/en-us/azure/azure-monitor/agents/agent-windows`)

- Active Directory (`https://docs.microsoft.com/en-us/azure/active-directory/fundamentals/active-directory-whatis`)

Utilize Azure Monitor

You can view your Azure Virtual Desktop service usage and its availability with Azure Monitor. You can receive notifications by configuring service health alerts for Azure Virtual Desktop. The following link provides further information on the Azure Monitor service: `https://azure.microsoft.com/services/monitor/`.

Utilize RemoteApps

There are two deployment model options with Azure Virtual Desktop—providing access to a full virtual desktop or to specific apps. You can deliver a seamless experience with remoteapps and reduce risk, as you are only exposing the specific application instead of a full Windows OS desktop.

This section discussed Azure Virtual Desktop security best practices. In the following section we look at specific session host security best practices.

Security Best Practices: Session Hosts

Session hosts are made up of Windows-based virtual machines that are connected to a virtual network. All these resources then sit in an Azure Subscription, which allows you to integrate Azure Virtual Desktop with several other security services.

The security of this environment is dependent on the controls and policies that are implemented on the session hosts. The following components should be integrated with this platform to ensure you are following best practices.

Endpoint Detection and Response

As with an on-premises computer, it is a recommendation that you deploy some type of endpoint protection software that has endpoint detection and response (EDR) capabilities on your session hosts. If you are deploying a Windows Server OS onto your session hosts, you can enable Azure Security Center (`https://docs.microsoft.com/en-us/azure/security-center/security-center-services`). You can also enable EDR, which will implement Defender ATP.

Endpoint Protection

It is a recommendation to enable endpoint protection on each session host. You have the choice of configuring a third-party tool or enabling Windows Defender Anti-Virus.

Patch Management

In the scenario in which a vulnerability has been identified, you have to ensure you patch it. The same rule should be utilized when managing virtual cloud environments like Azure Virtual Desktop. You should ensure that you have a reliable, strict, and robust patch-management policy for your environment that covers the OS and any applications on the session hosts.

This section discussed Azure Virtual Desktop security best practices and session host security best practices. In the next session, we take a closer look at securing Windows Virtual Desktop environments with Azure Security Center integration.

Azure Security Center Integration with AVD

Azure Security Center offers the following capabilities that cover the security posture and threat protection for Azure Virtual Desktop virtual machines:

- Adaptive application controls

- Secure score assessment

- Secure configuration assessment

- Vulnerability assessment

- Just-in-time (JIT) virtual machine access

- File integrity monitoring

- Host-level detections

- Agentless cloud network micro-segmentation and detections

Table 4-3 outlines the Azure Virtual Desktop security requirements and the Azure Security Center security and threat protection capabilities associated with it.

Table 4-3. *Azure Virtual Desktop Security Requirements*

Azure Virtual Desktop Requirements	Azure Security Center Security Capabilities	Azure Security Center Threat Protection Capabilities
Identity	Configuration assessment and secure score	Agentless cloud network micro-segmentation and detection
Network Security	Just-in-time (JIT) VM access Configuration assessment and secure score	Agentless cloud network micro-segmentation and detection
App Security	Vulnerability assessment File integrity monitoring Adaptive application control	Host-level detections
Configuration	Secure configuration assessment Secure score assessment	N/A
Session Host OS	Vulnerability assessment	Host-level detection

This section looked at the different security requirements for Azure Virtual Desktop and security best practices for session hosts. The next section includes a lab exercise that you use to enable Azure Security Center for Azure Virtual Desktop.

Enabling Azure Security Center for Azure Virtual Desktop

There are two tiers of Azure Security Center—the free tier and the standard tier. The free tier offers security suggestions and Secure Score for Azure Virtual Desktop; however, for this lab exercise, you need the standard tier.

The following lab exercise walks through enabling Azure Security Center for Azure Virtual Desktop:

1. Navigate to the Security Center service page by typing **Security Center** in the Azure Search bar at the top of the screen, as shown in Figure 4-24.

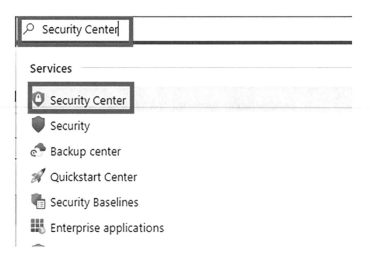

Figure 4-24. *Navigate to Azure Security Center*

2. Ensure the Standard Tier plan is enabled by navigating to Security
    Center ➤ Settings and clicking your trial subscription. See
    Figure 4-25.

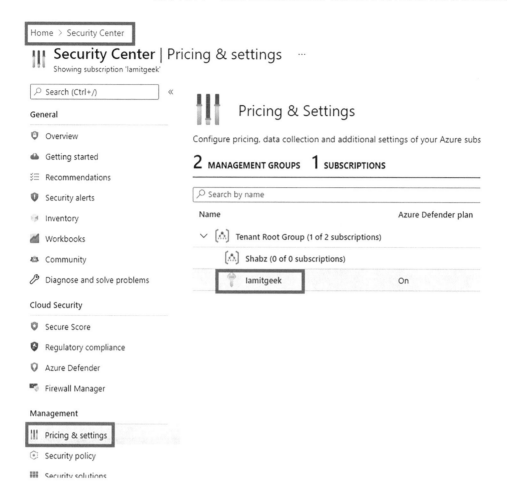

Figure 4-25. *Check Security Center Standard tier is enabled*

You should see the same detail as in Figure 4-26, which will confirm it is enabled.

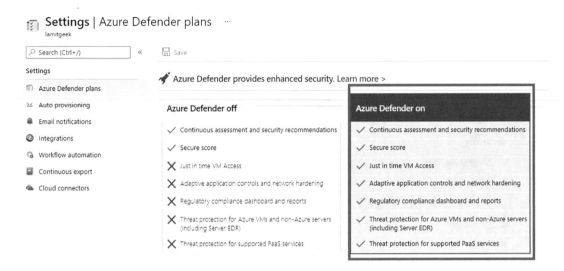

Figure 4-26. *Ensure Standard Tier is enabled*

3. You now need to enable threat protection for the virtual machine/ servers, as shown in Figure 4-27.

∧ Select Azure Defender plan by resource type   **Enable all**

Azure Defender for	Resource Quantity	Pricing	Plan	
Servers	1 servers	$15/Server/... ⓘ	On	Off
App Service	0 instances	$15/instanc... ⓘ	On	Off
Azure SQL Databases	0 servers	$15/Server/... ⓘ	On	Off
SQL servers on machi...	0 servers	$15/Server/... ⓘ $0.015/Core/t	On	Off
Open-source relation...	0 servers	$15/Server/... ⓘ	On	Off
Storage	2 storage accounts	$0.02/10k tr... ⓘ	On	Off
Kubernetes	0 kubernetes cores	$2/VM core... ⓘ	On	Off
Container registries	0 container registries	$0.29/Image	On	Off
Key Vault	0 key vaults	$0.02/10k transactions	On	Off
Resource Manager		$4/1M reso... ⓘ	On	Off
DNS		$0.7/1M D... ⓘ	On	Off

Figure 4-27. *Enable threat protection*

This section discussed Azure security integration with Azure Virtual Desktop. You also completed a lab exercise to enable it in the Azure Portal. You can now move on to the knowledge check to ensure you have understood the information in this chapter.

Knowledge Check

The following questions are aimed at testing your understanding of the information in this chapter. It is recommended that you complete all sections and labs in this chapter before attempting these questions.

Check Your Knowledge

1. You have been asked to give read-only access to a helpdesk team member to the Azure Virtual Desktop session hosts. Which built-in role should you grant access to? This must follow the Least Privilege Access model:

   - Desktop Virtualization Hostpool Reader

   - Desktop Virtualization Application Group Contributor

   - Desktop Virtualization Hostpool Contributor

2. Which of the following Azure Virtual Desktop services are managed by Microsoft? Choose three correct answers.

   - Web Access

   - Policies for Scaling

   - Diagnostics

   - Broker

   - End User Profile Management

3. Which of the following Azure Virtual Desktop services are managed by the end client? Choose three correct answers.

   - Gateway

   - End User Host Access

- Virtual Machine Scaling & Sizing

- Infrastructure Services

- Policies for Scaling

4. Which three Azure AD roles allow you to create and manage
   Conditional Access Policies?

- Global Administrator

- Helpdesk Administrator

- Security Administrator

- Conditional Access Administrator

- Intune Administrator

5. What Azure Security Center tier is required to integrate with Azure
   Virtual Desktop?

- Premium

- Free

- Standard

- Basic

Summary

This chapter looked at managing access and security to Azure Virtual Desktop, including managing access to Azure Virtual Desktop and managing security in Azure Virtual Desktop.

Chapter 5 takes a deep dive into managing user environments and apps, including implementing and managing FSLogix, configuring user experience settings, and installing and configuring apps on a session host.

CHAPTER 5

Manage User Environments and Apps

The previous chapter took a deeper look into managing access and security to Azure Virtual Desktop, including managing access to Azure Virtual Desktop and managing security for Azure Virtual Desktop.

This chapter covers the following main topics:

- Implement and manage FSLogix

- Configure user experience settings

- Install and configure apps on a session host

- Knowledge check

Technical Requirements

To complete the exercises in this book, you need to have access to a Microsoft 365 tenant. This can be attained by signing up for a trial subscription. Additionally, Azure Virtual Desktop services require one of the following licenses:

- Microsoft 365 Business Premium

- Microsoft 365 E5/E3

- Microsoft 365 A3/A5/Student Benefits

- Microsoft 365 F3

- Windows 10 Enterprise E3/E5

- Windows 10 Education A3/A5

- Windows 10 VDA per user

© Shabaz Darr 2022
S. Darr, *Azure Virtual Desktop Specialist*, https://doi.org/10.1007/978-1-4842-7987-8_5

Implementing and Managing FSLogix

This section discusses what FSLogix is and how it integrates with Azure Virtual Desktop (AVD). The lab exercises in this section show you how to configure FSLogix with AVD and migrate data from a local file share into Azure Storage.

What Is FSLogix?

FSLogix is tool that can be used in a variety of ways. The FSLogix solution can enrich, enable, and streamline non-persistent environments, especially with Windows and within Azure. FSLogix allows you to do the following:

- Preserve user data in non-persistent ecosystems

- Speed up login times for non-persistent ecosystems

- Boost input/output (IO) on files between session hosts and roaming profiles

- Give users who log in a local profile experience to minimize potential compatibility problems with redirection

- Manage images and applications easily

FSLogix can be utilized in several scenarios, including profile containers, office containers, application masking, and Java version control.

FSLogix Key Capabilities

FSLogix can be implemented in many use cases. The following are some of its key capabilities:

- FSLogix can relay end user profiles to a location that is available on the network. Mounting this profile and utilizing it over the network can minimize the risk of slow logins and delays that are historically associated with roaming profiles.

- With Office containerization, you can redirect the part of the profile that contains the Microsoft Office data only. This will enable you to have a better experience when using Microsoft Office in the Azure Virtual Desktop environment.

- FSLogix utilizes a filter driver to redirect the profile. This ensures that applications do not see that the profile is on a network drive. Some applications can have issues if they see that data is stored on a remote network, so this capability is very important.

- FSLogix profiles can integrate with Cloud Cache to make a robust and highly available ecosystem. We cover Cloud Cache integration later in this chapter.

- Access to applications, fonts, printers, and other elements is managed by application masking. Image management is significantly simplified by utilizing application masking.

FSLogix Licensing Requirements

There is a licensing requirement with FSLogix that you need to be aware of when planning your Azure Virtual Desktop deployments. FSLogix works with the following licenses:

- Microsoft 365 E3/E5

- Microsoft 365 A3/A5/Student Use Benefits

- Microsoft 365 F1/F3

- Microsoft 365 Business

- Windows 10 Enterprise E3/E5

- Windows 10 Education A3/A5

- Windows 10 VDA per user

- Remote Desktop Services (RDS) Client Access License (CAL)

- Remote Desktop Services (RDS) Subscriber Access License (SAL)

- Azure Virtual Desktop per-user access license

FSLogix is supported on Microsoft operating systems newer than Window 7 (Desktop, Windows Server 2008 Server) and supports 32-bit and 64-bit architectures.

Azure Virtual Desktop uses FSLogix integration to manage end user profiles, specifically the more personal elements, such as desktop settings, application settings, and any static network connections.

Azure Virtual Desktop uses FSLogix contained profiles to:

- Isolate user profiles from virtual machines (VMs)

- Facilitate a roaming profile experience using virtual hard disks (VHDs) stored in Azure Storage, Storage Spaces Direct, or Azure NetApp files

- Dynamically attach VHDs to end users

The FSLogix contained user profile is comparable to the classic roaming user profile you get with traditional Remote Desktop Services (RDS), in that the user profile and data is isolated from the Windows session. From an end user perspective, it feels like the data and information is stored locally on the Windows VM.

You saw Figure 5-1 in Chapter 3, when we were discussing Azure Storage, and it outlines the flow and process that is completed when getting the user profile after the user logs in to the AVD remote desktop client.

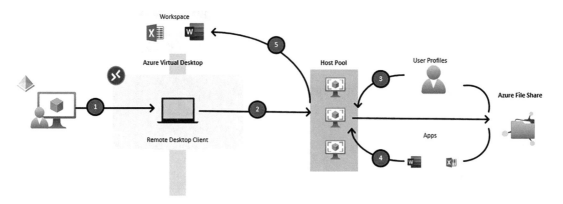

Figure 5-1. *Process of getting a user profile*

As a reminder, the diagram shows the following steps:

1. End user logs in to the remote desktop client with their Azure AD credentials (email address).

2. The user is logged in/assigned to a session host (VM).

3. The session host obtains the user's profile from the Azure File share.

4. When you have MSIX App Attach configured (see the section entitled "Using MSIX App Attach" later in this chapter), applications are dynamically sent to the VMs. FSLogix storage concepts are used in this scenario.

5. The end user's Azure Virtual Desktop workspace is filled with the applications that have been assigned to them or their session desktop.

If you followed Chapter 3, you completed the lab exercise in which we walked through the configuration of FSLogix. We don't repeat those steps in detail, but the following is a high-level explanation of what you need to do when provisioning FSLogix:

- Step 1: Create an Azure Storage account with Premium storage.

- Step 2: Create an Azure File share (SMB).

- Step 3: Domain-join the Azure Storage account to your Active Directory Domain Controller.

- Step 4: Install FSLogix on your virtual machine or session host image.

- Step 5: Configure the FSLogix profile container registry.

- Step 6: Assign the include and exclude user groups.

The section covered an introduction to FSLogix and discussed the high-level steps for provisioning FSLogix. The lab exercise in Chapter 3 showed you how to configure and deploy FSLogix with an Azure Storage account. The next section includes a lab exercise on configuring Cloud Cache to redirect profile containers or office containers to different providers.

Configuring Cloud Cache

Cloud Cache utilizes a local profile to help with the reads from a redirected profile and office container. Cloud Cache also enables you to utilize two locations to store information, which are constantly kept up to date when a user is logged in to a session.

Configure Cloud Cache for SMB: Profile Containers

When configuring Cloud Cache for profile containers, all the settings are applied in the registry key shown in Figure 5-2.

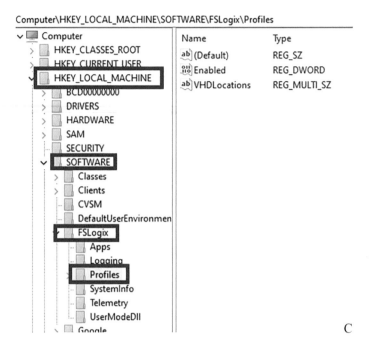

Figure 5-2. Profile container registry key location

1. First remove any registry setting for VHDLocations.

2. You now need to add the entries listed in Table 5-1 (or verify that they are in place).

Table 5-1. Profile Container Registry Value Information

Registry Value	Type	Value
CCDLocations	REG_SZ / MULTI_ SZ	Type=smb,connectionString=<\Location1\Folder1>;type= smb,connectionString=<\Location2\Folder2>
Enabled	DWORD	1

In this example, we separate each provider with a semicolon (;) and have two SMB providers. You need to specify the location for the Cloud Cache provider in between the braces (< and >).

Configure Cloud Cache for SMB: Office Containers

When configuring Cloud Cache for office containers, all settings are applied in the registry key shown in Figure 5-3.

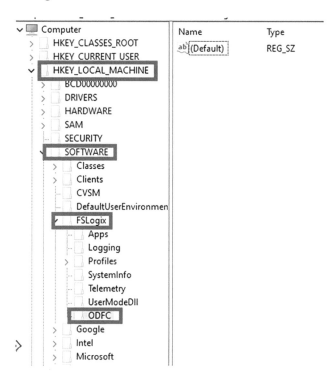

Figure 5-3. *Office container registry location*

1. First remove any registry setting for VHDLocations.

2. You now need to add the entries listed in Table 5-2 (or verify that they are in place).

Table 5-2. *Office Container Registry Information*

Registry Value	Type	Value
CCDLocations	REG_SZ / MULTI_SZ	type=smb,connectionString=<\Location1\Folder1>;type= smb,connectionString=<\Location2\folder2>
Enabled	DWORD	1

In this example, we separate each provider with a semicolon (;) and have two SMB providers. You need to specify the location for the Cloud Cache provider in between the braces (< and >).

Configure Cloud Cache: Azure Page Blobs

It is important to note that the following information and instructions should be used for testing and non-production environments. These steps shown in this section are only to be used to gain an understanding of Cloud Cache integration with Azure Page Blobs.

The steps outlined in this section expose very sensitive information, including Azure credentials, which is a huge security risk in a production environment. If you want to implement this in a production environment, you need to protect the credentials by utilizing Credential Manager at `https://docs.microsoft.com/en-us/fslogix/configure-cloud-cache-tutorial?WT.mc_id=modinfra-17152-thmaure#protect-azure-key-with-credential-manager`.

When configuring Cloud Cache for Azure Page Blob profile containers, all settings are applied in the registry key shown in Figure 5-4.

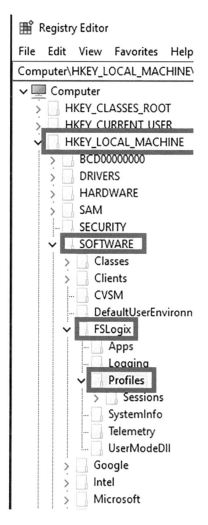

Figure 5-4. *Azure Page Blob profile container registry location*

1. First remove any registry setting for VHDLocations.

2. You now need to add the entries listed in Table 5-3 (or verify that they are in place).

Table 5-3. *Azure Page Blog Profile Container Registry Value Information*

Registry Value	Type	Value
CCDLocations	REG_SZ / MULTI_SZ	type=azure,connectionString="DefaultEndpointsProtocol=https;AccountName=;AccountKey=;EndpointSuffix="
Enabled	DWORD	1

In this example, we separate each provider with a semicolon (;) and have one Azure Page Blob provider. You need to specify the location for the Cloud Cache provider in between the braces (< and >). You also need to enter the Page Blob connection string in between the quotes (" and "). The following settings are used to create the Azure connection string:

- `DefaultEndpointsProtocol={http or https]`

- `AccountName=myAccountName`

- `AccountKey=myAccountKey`

- `EndpointSuffix=mySuffix`

You can find the payload for the connection string by navigating to Storage Accounts ➤ Settings ➤ Access Keys, as shown in Figure 5-5.

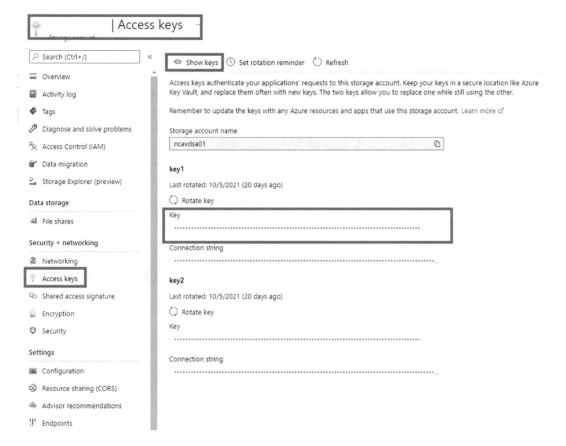

Figure 5-5. *Payload connection location*

When configuring Cloud Cache for Azure Page Blob office containers, all settings are applied in the registry key shown in Figure 5-6.

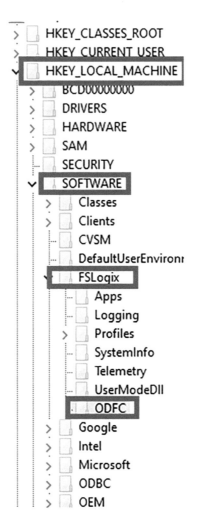

Figure 5-6. *Azure Page Blob office container registry location*

1. First remove any registry setting for VHDLocations.

2. You now need to add the entries listed in Table 5-4 (or verify that they are in place).

Table 5-4. *Azure Blob Container Registry Entries*

Registry Value	Type	Value
CCDLocations	REG_SZ / MULTI__SZ	type=smb,connectionString=<\FILESERVER\Shared Folder>;type=azure,connectionString="DefaultEnd pointsProtocol=https;AccountName=;AccountKey=; EndpointSuffix="
Enabled	DWORD	1

In this example, we separate each provider with a semicolon (;) and have one Azure Page Blob provider. You need to specify the location for the Cloud Cache provider in between the braces (< and >). You also need to enter the Page Blob connection string in between the quotes (" and "). The following settings are used to create the Azure connection string.

- `DefaultEndpointsProtocol={http or https]`

- `AccuntName=myAccountName`

- `AccountKey=myAccountKey`

- `EndpointSuffix=mySuffix`

This section discussed Cloud Cache integration with FSLogix and explained how to configure profile, office, and Azure Page Blob containers. The next section covers a few different methods for migrating user profiles to FSLogix.

Migrating Files in Azure Storage

Once you have provisioned the relevant storage and user profiles as part of the Azure Virtual Desktop (AVD), in some cases you may need to migrate user data from their on-premises user profiles or other locations into Azure Storage.

You can utilize Azure File Sync to synchronize shares on on-premises file servers into your Azure Storage, specifically the Azure Files shares you created for the user profiles. The following lab walks through the steps you need to follow to deploy Azure File Sync.

Deploy Azure File Sync

Before starting the deployment, you need to ensure you have completed the following prerequisites:

1. Provision an Azure File share in the same region you want to create the Azure File Sync. In this example, that would be UK South.

2. A Windows Server to sync with Azure File Sync.

Once these prerequisites are met, you need to prepare the Windows Server you want to utilize with Azure File Sync:

1. Log in to your on-premises server with an account that has the relevant admin privileges. Open Server Manager and then click Local Server, as shown in Figure 5-7.

Figure 5-7. *Navigate to the local server in Server Manager*

2. Click the IE Enhanced Security Configuration link on the properties page, as shown in Figure 5-8.

Last installed updates	Today at 10:05
Windows Update	Install updates automatically using Windows Update
Last checked for updates	Today at 10:05
Windows Defender Antivirus	Real-Time Protection: On
Feedback & Diagnostics	Settings
IE Enhanced Security Configuration	Off
Time zone	(UTC+00:00) Dublin, Edinburgh, Lisbon, London
Product ID	00430-00000-00000-AA829 (activated)

Figure 5-8. *IE Enhanced Security Configuration*

3. You need to select Off on the Internet Explorer Enhanced Security Configuration windows that opens, as shown in Figure 5-9.

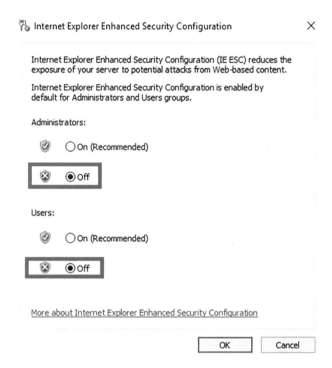

Figure 5-9. *Turn Internet Explorer Enhanced Security Configuration off*

4. Log in to the Azure Portal with a global admin account at `https://portal.azure.com`.

5. Select Create a Resource and search for the Azure File Sync service. Click it and then select Create. See Figure 5-10.

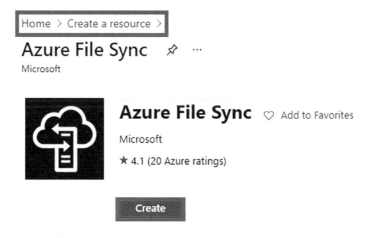

Figure 5-10. *Create the Azure Sync resource in the Azure Portal*

6. On the Basics page, fill out the following information
    (see Figure 5-11):

    - Subscription

    - Resource Group

    - Storage Sync Service Name

    - Region

Home > Create a resource > Azure File Sync >

Deploy Azure File Sync   ⋯

Azure File Sync in combination with Azure file shares allows you to centralize your organization's file shares in Azure, while keeping the flexibility, performance, and compatibility of an on-premises file server. Learn more

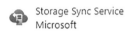 Storage Sync Service
Microsoft

Deploying this storage sync service resource will allow you to transform your Windows Server into a quick cache for Azure file shares with optional cloud tiering and multi-server sync functionality. Keep in mind that servers registered to different storage sync service resources cannot exchange data with each other. It's best to register all servers to the same storage sync service if they will ever have a need to sync the same Azure file share.

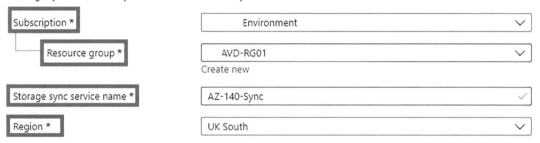

Figure 5-11. *Azure File Sync Basics tab*

7. You can add any relevant tags and then validate the configuration before completing the creation.

8. You now need to install the Azure File Sync agent onto the Windows Server VM. You can download the agent at `https://go.microsoft.com/fwlink/?linkid=858257`.

9. Once you have downloaded the agent onto the Windows Server and started the installation process, it is recommended you do the following:

   • Keep the default installation path as it is.

   • Enable Microsoft updates to ensure the Azure File Sync agent is kept up to date.

Register the Windows Server with the Storage Sync Service

Once the installation is completed, you will find that the Server Registration user interface (UI) opens automatically. Follow these steps to complete the registration process:

1. Sign in to the registration window with your Azure admin account.

2. Enter the following information:

   • Azure subscription that contains the Azure File Sync deployment

   • Resource group that contains the Azure File Sync

   • Enter a name for the Storage Sync service that will be registered

3. Click Register. During the registration process, you will need to enter your sign-in credentials a few more times.

Create a Sync Group and Cloud Endpoint

The final step in this implementation is to create a sync group and a cloud endpoint. The sync group identifies the sync topology for the files. At least one sync endpoint must exist within a sync group, which signifies an Azure File share and a server endpoint. The following steps outline how to provision the sync group:

1. Navigate to the Storage Sync service in the Azure Portal.

2. On the Overview page, click + Sync Group.

3. Enter the following information:

   • A sync group name

   • The subscription you use to deploy the Storage Sync service

   • The Azure Storage account name

   • The name of the Azure File share you want to sync with

Create a Server Endpoint

After the sync group has been successfully provisioned, you can add the server endpoint.

1. Navigate to the sync group and click Add Server Endpoint.

2. Enter the following information to create the server endpoint:

    - The name of the server you want to configure as the server endpoint.

    - The Windows server path you want to be synchronized for the sync group.

    - Enable or disable Cloud Tiering. With this enabled, files that are infrequently accessed can be tiered to the Azure File share.

    - Specify the amount of free disk space you want to reserve on the volume that's on the server endpoint.

    - Specify the initial download mode. This is optional.

This section looked at what FSLogix is and described its components, as well as explained the Azure File Sync tool that you can implement to manage migrations from on-premises server shares to Azure files. The next section takes a closer look at configuring user experience settings.

Configuring User Experience Settings

An important part of Azure Virtual Desktop (AVD) is to ensure the user experience is positive and that users can complete all the same job functions they do on a physical laptop from within the AVD sessions. The section explores the various user experience settings, including Universal Print, managing settings via group policies and Endpoint Manager, remote desktop protocol (RDP) properties, and troubleshooting issues with AVD and user profiles.

Universal Print

Before configuring Universal Print and discussing what is required, you need to understand what it is. Universal Print is an innovative Microsoft solution for printing used to manage printing systems via cloud services. This service is hosted fully in Azure and does not require any on-premises integration when deployed with Universal Print-compatible printers.

This service does require a Microsoft subscription that is supported with the following subscriptions:

- Microsoft 365 Enterprise F3, E3, E5, A3, A5

- Windows 10 Enterprise E3, E5, A3, A5

- Microsoft 365 Business Premium

There is a standalone subscription available for people without a subscription that includes Universal Print, but it does not come with Azure Active Directory, which is a requirement for this service.

Figure 5-12 shows the architecture and components that make up the Universal Print service. Table 5-5 covers each component in further detail.

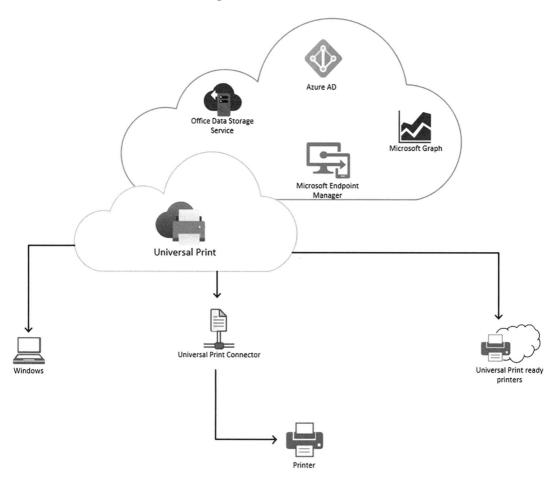

Figure 5-12. *Universal Print architecture*

Table 5-5. *Universal Print Architecture Components*

Component	Description
Universal Print	Cloud print service
Azure Active Directory	User and device identity and authorization service
Office Data Storage Service	Print queue data storage service
Microsoft Endpoint Manager	Client device printer provisioning policy service
Microsoft Graph	Printer management API
Universal Print Connector	A component that handles communication between printers and the Universal Print service
Universal Print ready printer	A printer that has built-in support for communicating with Universal Print
Printer without Native UP support	A printer that needs to be registered using the Universal Print Connector to communicate with Universal Print

Now that you understand what Universal Print is and have seen some of the components that work together to create this service, complete the next lab exercise to configure it.

Deploy Universal Print

Before you can complete configuration steps, you need to ensure the following prerequisites are met:

- Assign the relevant license to the standard user who will be using the printer (see earlier in this section for a list of supported licenses).

- Assign the relevant license to the Administrator account that will be configuring this service (see earlier in this section for a list of supported licenses).

- Ensure the Administrator account has the relevant access rights. The account must have one of the following two Azure Active Directory (Azure AD) roles:

  - Printer Administrator

  - Global Administrator

- Ensure you have a Windows operating system (OS) client device with at least version 1903 or higher OS build installed. This device is the one you intend to print from Universal Print.

- Ensure the device you want to print from has Internet access.

The first step is to set up the Universal Print Connector. This is a component that you use to enable the printer to work with the Universal Print service. The only time you do not use this is if you have a printer that can directly connect with the Universal Print service.

The connector has three main functions:

- It allows the administrator to register printers with the Universal Print Service.

- It sends reports on print job status and printer status to the Universal Printer Service.

- It retrieves print jobs from the Universal Print Service and sends them directly to the printer.

To check if the license assignment has Universal Print enabled, follow these steps:

1. Log in to `https://portal.azure.com` with an account that has privileges to assign licenses. In this scenario, we can use a global admin account.

2. Navigate to Azure Active Directory ➤ Licenses ➤ All products, as shown in Figure 5-13.

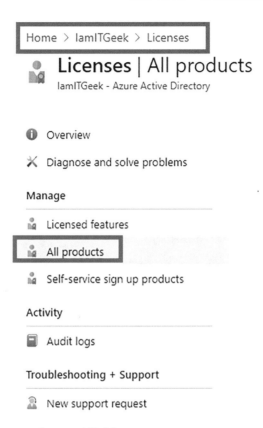

Figure 5-13. *Navigate to Azure AD Licenses*

3. Click the relevant license in the center pane and ensure the tick
    box is selected. Then click + Assign, as shown in Figure 5-14.

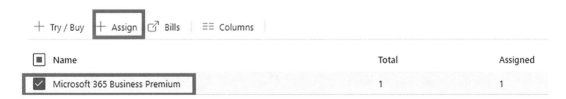

Figure 5-14. *Select the relevant license*

4. On the Assign License page, click Assignment Options and find
    the Universal Print option in the list of features. This needs to be
    toggled to On, as shown in Figure 5-15.

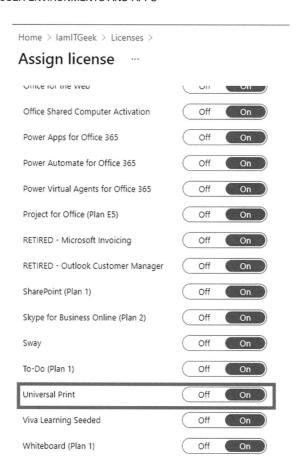

Figure 5-15. Turn on Universal Print in the License features

5. At the bottom of the page, click Review + Assign, as shown in
   Figure 5-16.

Figure 5-16. Review and assign license

6. Click Assign to complete this task.

In the next set of steps, you need to download and install the connector software on
the server you are using as your Print Server.

7. Download the Universal Print Connector software from `https://aka.ms/UPConnector`. (Note this is a direct download so run it on the print server.)

8. Save the installer locally on the server. Right-click the file and choose Run as Administrator, as shown in Figure 5-17.

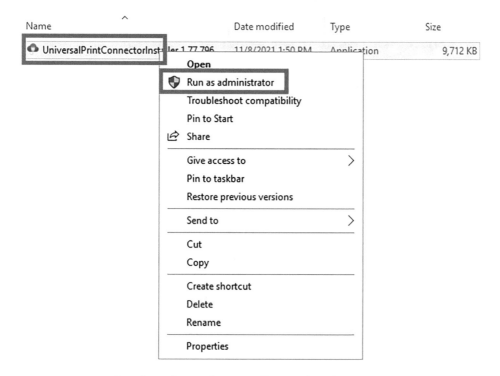

Figure 5-17. *Download and run the installer with Administrator rights*

9. Agree to the license terms and conditions and click Install; see Figure 5-18.

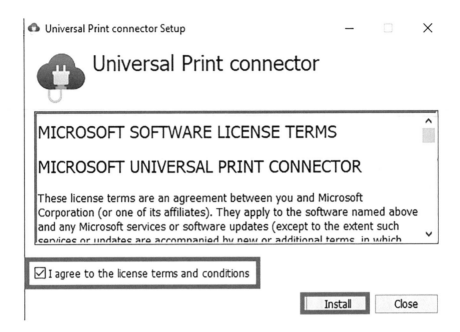

Figure 5-18. *Agree to the terms and conditions and install*

10. Once the installation is completed, the window will show the
    message "Setup Successful" (see Figure 5-19). Click Close.

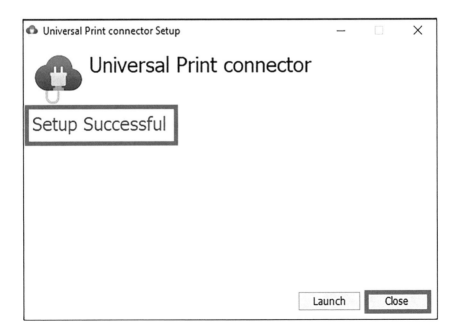

Figure 5-19. *Setup completed; click close*

11. You will now see the PrintConnectorApp on the desktop, as shown in Figure 5-20. Double-click this app to start the connector.

Figure 5-20. *PrintConnectorApp icon*

12. You will see a warning pop up on the screen that explains that the connector is going to collect data. Click OK to close this warning box, as shown in Figure 5-21.

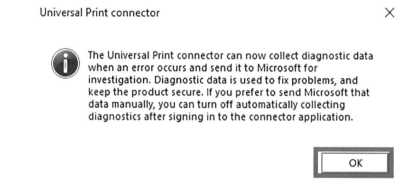

Figure 5-21. *Warning about the Universal Print service collecting data*

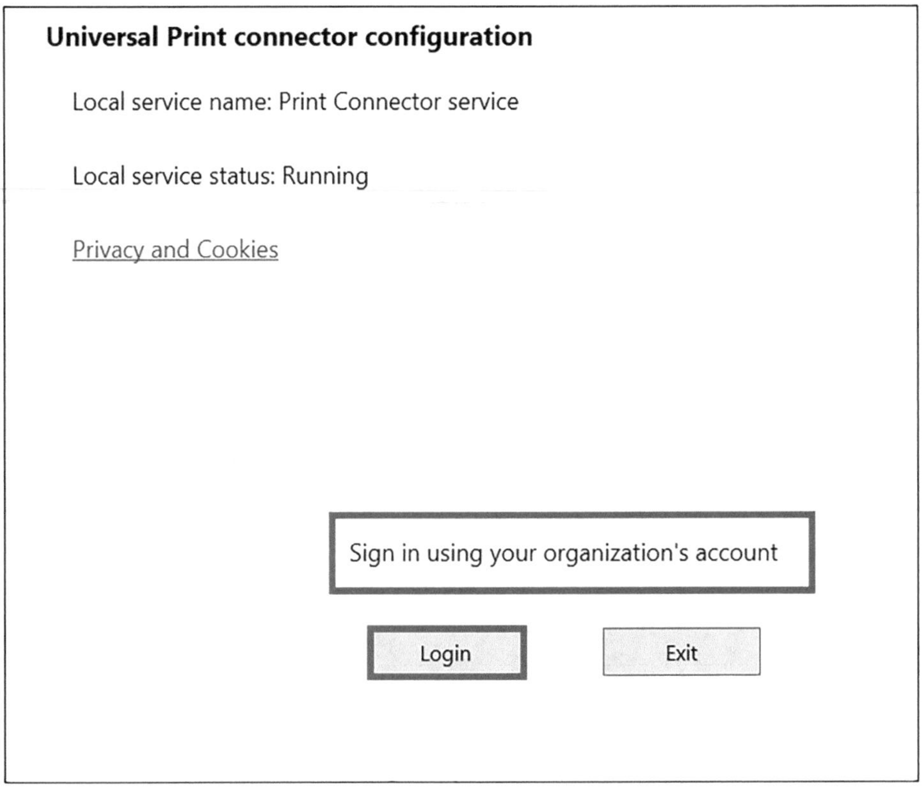

Universal Print connector configuration

Local service name: Print Connector service

Local service status: Running

Privacy and Cookies

Sign in using your organization's account

| Login | Exit |

Figure 5-22. *Log in using global admin credentials*

13. From the Universal Print Connector window, click Login and enter an account with print administrator or global administrator credentials. For this lab, we use global admin credentials.

14. Once you have logged in, you need to add the connecter name in the text field at the bottom of the window and click Register. See Figure 5-23.

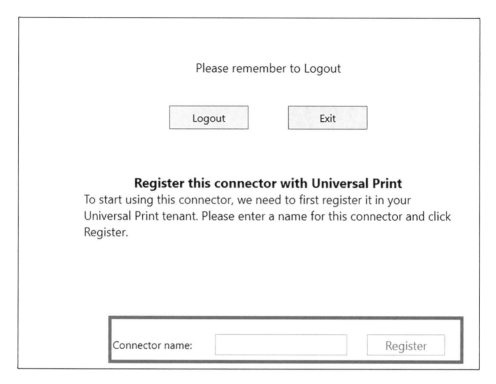

Figure 5-23. *Register the new connector*

15. You should now be able to see the connector in the Universal Print Portal. Navigate to the Universal Print Portal by typing ***Universal Print*** in the search box at the top of the Azure Portal, as shown in Figure 5-24.

Figure 5-24. *Navigate to the Universal Print Portal*

16. Once you are at the Universal Print Portal, click Connectors in the left pane to verify that your connector has been registered, as shown in Figure 5-25.

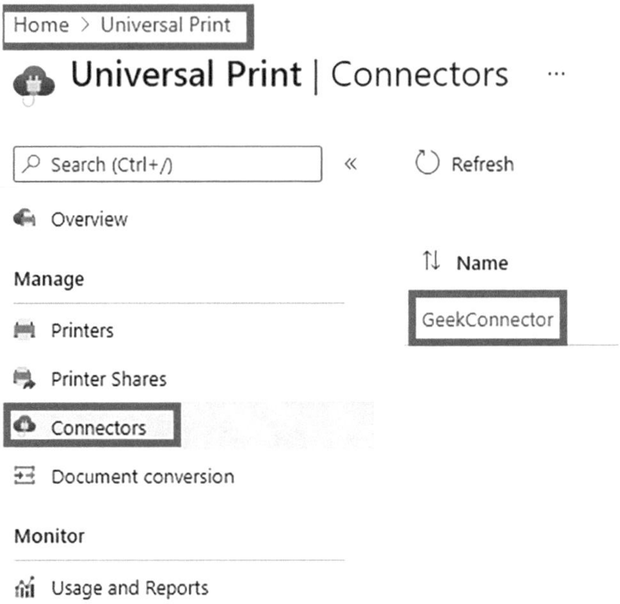

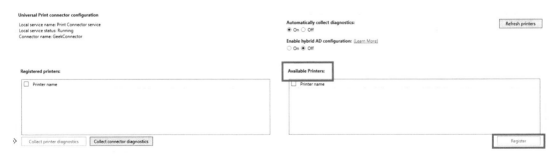

Figure 5-25. Confirm connector registration

If you flip back to the Universal Print Connector app you installed on the server earlier, you can start to register printers. Note that you can only register printers that are available locally from the server you have installed the print connector on.

17. You should see the available printers in the Available Printers section. You can highlight the one you want to register and click Register. See Figure 5-26.

Figure 5-26. Check available printers and register the ones you want to integrate with the Universal Print service

Now that you have successfully registered the printers, you need to share and assign users the permission to print to them.

18.   Navigate back to the Universal Print Portal within Azure and click Printers in the left pane, as shown in Figure 5-27.

Figure 5-27. *Navigate to Printers in the Universal Printer Portal*

19.   You should see all the registered printers in the middle window pane. However, they will appear as Not Shared under the Share Status, as shown in Figure 5-28.

Figure 5-28. *Not shared status*

20.   To share the printer, check the box to the left of the printer's name and then click the Share button. See Figure 5-29.

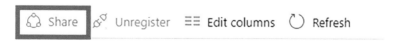

Figure 5-29. *Share the registered printers*

21. When sharing a printer, you can enter any relevant name for the
printer share and then select members you want to have access to
this printer. See Figure 5-30.

Share printers

Create a Printer Share to let your users find and use this printer.

Share name *

Allow access to everyone in my organization

Select member(s)

Selected members

Share Printer   Cancel

Figure 5-30. *Enter a share name and assign access to users*

You are now ready to add the printer to your Windows 10 test client.

22. Navigate to Start Menu ➤ Settings ➤ Devices ➤ Printers &
Scanners, as shown in Figure 5-31.

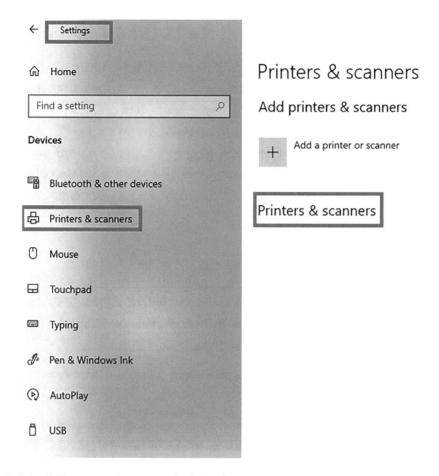

Figure 5-31. *Printers & Scanners in Windows 10*

Users who have been given permission to the Universal Printer during the sharing process will see the printer in their list, and those that have not been given access will not see it.

This section discussed the Universal Printer Service, including what it is and how it works. You then completed a lab exercise to configure and deploy the Universal Printer Service to a Windows 10 device. The next section looks at installing and configuring apps on session hosts.

Installing and Configuring Apps on a Session Host

You have several options for deploying applications with Azure Virtual Desktop, including installing them as part of your customized Windows image, publishing them via a RemoteApp application group, and using a packing tool called MSIX app to create a package of the application and attach it to your session via an Azure File share.

This section looks at deploying and managing apps with RemoteApp application groups, configuring application masking, implementing MSIX App Attach, implementing OneDrive for Business in a multi-session environment, and implementing Microsoft Teams in a VDI environment.

RemoteApp Application Groups

One of the many features of AVD is what's called an *application group*. This is essentially a logical grouping of apps that are installed on virtual machine session hosts in a hostpool. AVD has two types of application groups:

- **Desktop:** This allows users to access a fully published Windows desktop.

- **RemoteApp:** This enables users to access specific applications that are installed on the default Windows image but are published so you do not have to access the full desktop to use them.

Implement a RemoteApp Group

This section walks through steps in a lab to create a RemoteApp group.

1. Log in to the Azure Portal via a web browser from `https://portal.azure.com` using an account that has global admin credentials.

2. Navigate to the Azure Virtual Desktop service by typing it into the top search bar and selecting it from the options. See Figure 5-32.

Figure 5-32. *Navigate to the Azure Virtual Desktop service*

3. On the left pane, click Application Groups, as shown in
   Figure 5-33.

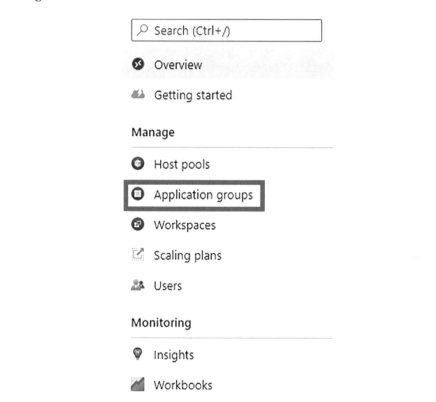

Figure 5-33. *Application Groups feature*

4. If you have existing application groups, you will see them in the list. Click + Create, as shown in Figure 5-34.

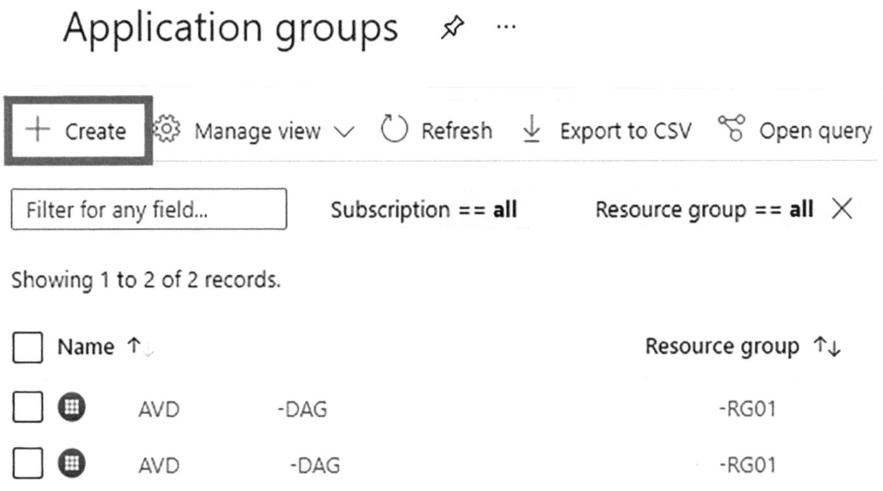

Figure 5-34. *Create a new application group*

5. In the Create an Application Group window, you need to enter the following information on the Basics tab and then click Next (see Figure 5-35):

- Subscription

- Resource group

- Hostpool you want to create the application group in

- Application group type (you need to select RemoteApp)

- Application group name

Create an application group ...

Basics   Applications   Assignments   Workspace   Advanced   Tags   Review + create

Subscription * ⓘ

Environment   ∨

Resource group * ⓘ

-RG01   ∨

Create new

Host pool * ⓘ

-AVD   -HP   ∨

Location ⓘ

UK South   ∨

ⓘ Metadata stored in same location as host pool

Application group type

RemoteApp application groups are where you can add applications. A Desktop application group will grant full desktop access.

Application group type * ⓘ

◉ RemoteApp   ◯ Desktop

ⓘ A desktop App group already exists in the selected host pool and you can only create RemoteApp app groups. Learn more

Application group name *

AVD-140-App   ✓

Figure 5-35. *Basics tab when creating an Application Group*

6. Click + Add Applications on the Applications tab, as shown in Figure 5-36.

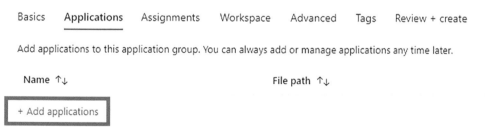

Basics   **Applications**   Assignments   Workspace   Advanced   Tags   Review + create

Add applications to this application group. You can always add or manage applications any time later.

Name ↑↓   File path ↑↓

+ Add applications

Figure 5-36. *Add an application*

7. In the Add Application window, you first need to select the
    application source. There are three options for this:

    - **Start Menu:** This uses the Start menu of the Windows session
      host to publish the application.

    - **File Path:** This uses the file path of the app's installation path on
      the Windows OS to publish the app.

    - **MSIX Package:** This uses a customized app package stored on an
      Azure File share to attach the app rather than publish it.

In this example, we use the Start Menu option, as shown in Figure 5-37.

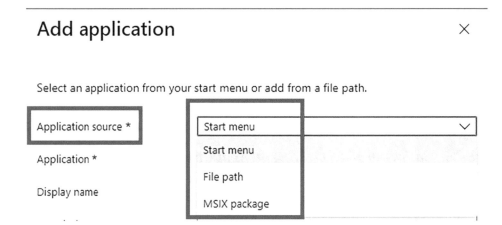

Figure 5-37. *Select an application source*

8. The rest of the options are as follows (see Figure 5-38):

    - **Application:** Select the app from the drop-down of all
      applications enabled on the Windows Start menu. In this
      example, we use Notepad.

    - **Display Name:** Give the app a relevant name or leave it as its
      default.

    - **Description:** Enter a description.

    - **Application Path:** This will be auto filled.

    - **Icon Path:** This will be auto filled.

    - *Icon Index:* This will be auto filled.

Click Next after you enter the options.

Select an application from your start menu or add from a file path.

Application source *	Start menu ⌄
Application *	Notepad ⌄
Display name	Notepad
Description	AZ-140 NotePad Lab
Application path ⓘ	C:\Windows\system32\notepad.exe
Icon path	C:\Windows\system32\notepad.exe
Icon index	0
Require command line	● No ○ Yes

Figure 5-38. *Enter the rest of the application settings*

9. On the Assignments tab, assign the relevant user or group to which you want to allow access to this RemoteApp group. Click Next.

10. On the Workspace tab, click Yes for Register Application Group. Ensure the correct workspace is selected in the drop-down box below it. See Figure 5-39. Click Next after you enter the options.

Basics   Applications   Assignments   **Workspace**   Advanced   Tags   Review + create

To save some time, you can register the default desktop application group from this host pool, with a new or pre-existing workspace.

Register application group   ○ No ● Yes

Register application group ⓘ   ▮WS01 ⌄

ⓘ Another application group in NC-AVD-MOD-HP has already been registered, so this app group will also be registered to that same workspace.

Figure 5-39. *Add your workspace*

11. On the Advanced tab, you can enable diagnostics or leave it as the default, as we do in this example. Click Next.

12. Create any relevant tags, then review and create the application group.

Once these steps are completed, log in to AVD via the remote desktop app with a user account you assigned to this RemoteApp. You will see a Notepad application that you can launch and start to use. This section discussed what a RemoteApp application group is and you completed a lab to implement it for AVD. The next section discusses FSLogix application masking and configures it as part of the lab exercise.

FSLogix Application Masking

Application masking is a feature of FSLogix that's utilized to manage access to installed applications. The software that allows you to manage this is called the Application Rules Editor, and it allows you to describe the application that you want to manage. You can additionally specify rules to manage by.

The Application Rules Editor has the following features:

- Create new rule sets

- Edit existing rule sets

- Manage user and group assignments for the rule sets

- Test rule sets

FSLogix supports four types of rule sets:

- **Hiding Rule:** This rule hides specified elements using specific criteria. See Figure 5-40.

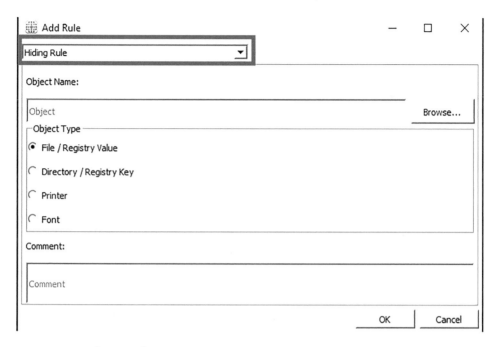

Figure 5-40. *Hiding Rule*

- **Redirection Rule:** This rule redirects the specific item as described. See Figure 5-41.

Figure 5-41. *Redirection Rule*

- **App Container Rule:** This rule redirects the specific information into a virtual hard disk (VHD). See Figure 5-42.

Figure 5-42. *App Container Rule*

- **Specify Value Rule:** The specified item is assigned a value. See Figure 5-43.

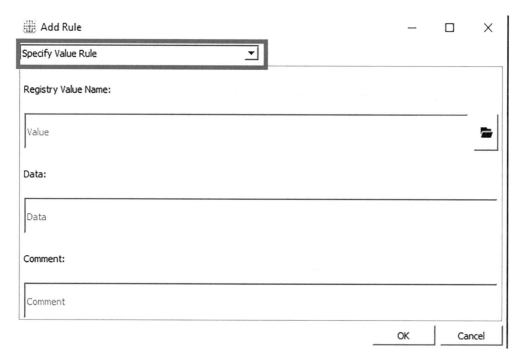

Figure 5-43. *Specify Value Rule*

The following lab exercise shows you how to create the first rule set with the FSLogix Rules Editor:

1. Download and install FSLogix and FSLogix Rules Editor onto your session host virtual machines (VMs). The direct download link is `https://aka.ms/fslogix/download`.

2. Navigate to the FSLogix Rules Editor software via the Windows Start menu, as shown in Figure 5-44.

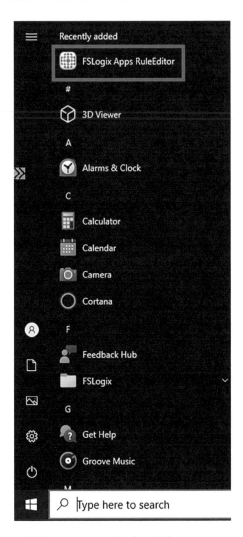

Figure 5-44. *Navigate to FSLogix Apps Rules Editor*

3. When the FSLogix Rules Editor opens, choose File ➤ New to create a new rule set. See Figure 5-45.

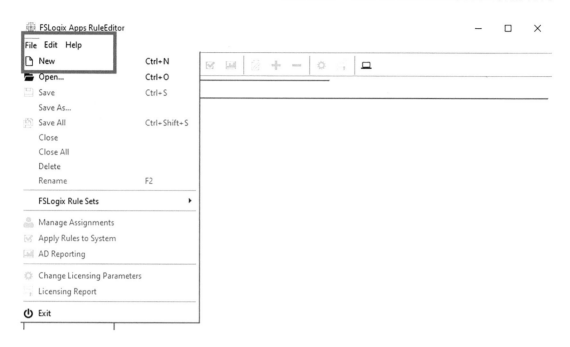

Figure 5-45. *Create a new file*

4.   Enter a file name and then click Enter File Name, as shown in
Figure 5-46.

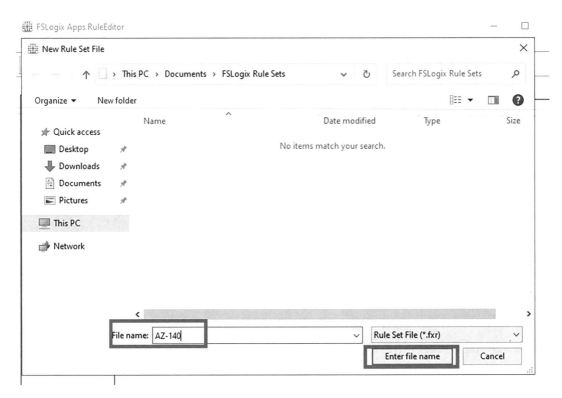

Figure 5-46. *Enter a file name for the new rule*

5. You need to select an application you want to manage. Browse to the installation directory and click Scan to allow the Rules Editor to pick up its settings. Click OK when scanning is complete. See Figure 5-47.

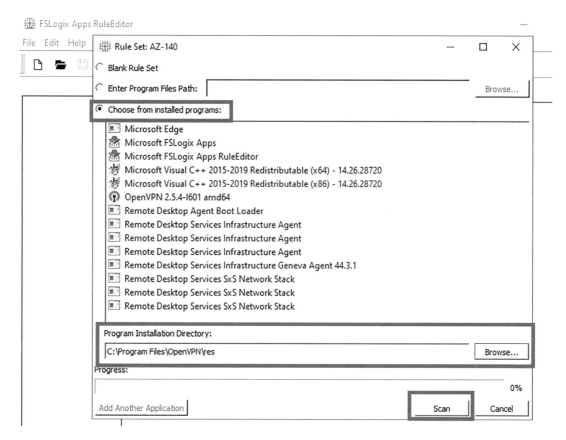

Figure 5-47. *Enter application details and run a scan*

6.   You should now see the specific rules explaining the items inside
the rule set. See Figure 5-48.

Figure 5-48. *Hidden Rule rule set*

You can now test your rule set and make assignments to it. To test your rule set:

7. Click your rule set in the left pane window.

8. Choose File ➤ Apply Rules to System.

9. This will apply the rules in your rule set to the session host. In this example, you should not see the application, as it will now be hidden.

    Assignments to the rule set show how the rules will be applied. To make assignments for this rule set:

10. Choose File ➤ Manage Assignment then click Add.

11. Select the type of assignment.

12. Enter the relevant information and click OK.

13. Choose if you want to Apply or Not Apply.

This section discussed application masking and you completed a lab exercise to implement it. The following section takes a closer look at dynamic app delivery by using MSIX App Attach.

Using MSIX App Attach

MSIX is a relatively new application packaging setup that has several features that provide an improved packaging experience. From an Azure Virtual Desktop perspective, MSIX App Attach can:

- Allow segregation of user information, the operating system, and applications by utilizing containers

- Allow for quicker login times for clients

- Minimize infrastructure and lower cost

- Remove any repackaging needs, as it delivers apps dynamically

The lab exercise for MSIX App Attach has a few different elements to it and is time consuming, so we will not cover it in detail in this chapter. However, we discuss the prerequisite tasks that need to be completed as well as share links to guides that can walk you through the deployment.

Before you start the lab exercise, you need to ensure the following prerequisite items are in place:

- A working AVD deployment.

- AVD hostpool with a minimum of one working session host.

- MSIX packaging tool. You can download this from the Windows Store on your Windows 10 test device.

- An Azure File share where you will store the MSIX package. This needs to be accessible.

- A certificate. The following link explains how you can achieve it: https://docs.microsoft.com/en-us/azure/virtual-desktop/app-attach#install-certificates.

The following link explains the steps you need to complete to create an MSIX package from the Desktop Installer: `https://docs.microsoft.com/en-us/windows/msix/packaging-tool/create-app-package`.

Once the package is created and uploaded to the file share that the session host VMs have access to, you can follow this link to set up MSIX App Attach with the Azure Portal: `https://docs.microsoft.com/en-us/azure/virtual-desktop/app-attach-azure-portal`.

This section explained what MSIX is, how it can integrate with AVD, and the benefits it enables. The next section discusses OneDrive for Business integration and Microsoft Teams integration with AVD.

Integrating OneDrive for Business with AVD

OneDrive for Business allows users to securely access files that are stored in the Microsoft Cloud from any location and using various devices. It also allows users to share these files internally and externally, depending on your company policy.

To integrate OneDrive for Business with Azure Virtual Desktop, you need to utilize the OneDrive Sync app on the session hosts. The per-machine installation option is new and provides the following:

- Automatic movement from the old version of the OneDrive for Business sync application (Groove.exe)

- Automatic transfer from the per-user to per-machine method

- Automatic updates when a new version is available

It supports OneDrive and SharePoint File Sync with SharePoint Server 2019 and Microsoft 365. The following steps outline how to deploy the Sync app:

1. Download `OneDriveSetup.exe` onto the session host.

2. From an elevated command prompt, run the `OneDriveSetup.exe /allusers` command from the folder you downloaded the .EXE file to.

Integrating Microsoft Teams with AVD

Microsoft Teams is a collaboration tool that integrates with Microsoft 365 and is used for instant messaging, video calls, document collaboration, and in some cases cloud telephony. If you want to utilize Microsoft Teams in a VDI environment such as Azure Virtual Desktop, you need the following elements:

- **Virtualization broker:** The resource and connection manager for the provider, in this case Azure.

- **Session host:** The VM that Microsoft Teams will run on.

- **Client device:** The endpoint the user connects the virtual desktop from.

- **Desktop app:** The Microsoft Teams Desktop client application.

The following link describes the steps you need to follow to implement Microsoft Teams in your AVD environment. It is recommended to complete this as a lab exercise: `https://docs.microsoft.com/en-us/azure/virtual-desktop/teams-on-avd`.

This section explained how to integrate OneDrive for Business and Microsoft Teams with Azure Virtual Desktop. You can now complete the knowledge check to finish off this chapter.

Knowledge Check

The following questions are aimed at testing your understanding of the information in this chapter. It is recommended that you complete all the sections and labs in this chapter before attempting to answer these questions.

Check Your Knowledge

1. Which Azure Storage type can you integrate with Cloud Cache:

   - Azure Files

   - Managed Disks

   - Azure Page Blobs

2. Which Azure Storage type can you integrate with FSLogix to containerize user profiles?

- Managed Disks

- Azure Files

- Azure Page Blobs

3. Which component handles communication between printers and the Universal Print service?

- Office Data Storage Service

- Universal Print Connector

- Microsoft Graph

Summary

This chapter looked at managing user environments and apps, including implementing and managing FSLogix, configuring user experience settings, and installing and configuring apps on a session host.

Chapter 6 takes a deep dive into monitoring and maintaining an Azure Virtual Desktop infrastructure, including implementing business continuity and DR, automating AVD management tasks, and monitoring performance and health.

Monitor and Maintain an Azure Virtual Desktop Infrastructure

The previous chapter took a deeper look into managing user environments and applications for Azure Virtual Desktop.

This chapter covers the following main topics:

- Planning and implementing business continuity and disaster recovery

- Automating Azure Virtual Desktop management tasks

- Monitoring and managing performance tasks

- Knowledge check

Technical Requirements

To complete the exercises in this book, you need access to a Microsoft 365 tenant. This can be attained by signing up for a trial subscription. Additionally, Azure Virtual Desktop services require one of the following licenses:

- Microsoft 365 Business Premium

- Microsoft 365 E5/E3

- Microsoft 365 A3/A5/Student Benefits

- Microsoft 365 F3

© Shabaz Darr 2022
S. Darr, *Azure Virtual Desktop Specialist*, https://doi.org/10.1007/978-1-4842-7987-8_6

213

- Windows 10 Enterprise E3/E5

- Windows 10 Education A3/A5

- Windows 10 VDA per user

Planning and Implementing Business Continuity and Disaster Recovery

There are many disasters that can affect an organization's infrastructure and its continuity. Just because your infrastructure is provisioned in the cloud, does not mean it cannot be affected by any number of disasters. This section looks at the different ways in which you can plan for these disasters and implement services alongside Azure Virtual Desktop (AVD) to facilitate Business Continuity Plans (BCPs).

Which Components Do You Need to Protect?

When planning and designing a BCP, you must first understand which components need to be included in that plan, and which components are not your responsibility. Chapter 2 looks at the AVD responsibility model, including which components are managed by Microsoft and which are managed by the consumer. A recap of that discussion follows.

The following components are managed by Microsoft:

- **Web Access:** This component enables the end user to gain access to AVD and the virtual applications via a HTML5-compatible Internet browser. This can be accessed from any device from anywhere as long as it has a secure Internet connection. To increase security, you can also utilize multi-factor authentication in Azure AD to control access to this component.

- **Connection Broker:** User connections to the remote desktop and remote applications are managed by this component of Azure Virtual Desktop. It delivers load balancing and reconnections to disconnected sessions.

- **Gateway:** This component allows remote users to connect to Azure Virtual Desktop resources from any device that is connected to the

Internet. The gateway coordinates a connection from the virtual machine back to the same gateway.

- **Extensibility Components:** AVD can be managed by utilizing Windows PowerShell or with the REST APIs that are provided, which also allows for support from third-party tools.

- **Diagnostics:** This event-based aggregator marks each action (made by a user or administrator) on the AVD deployment as a fail or success. It is then possible to query the event to discover failing components.

The following components are managed by you, the consumer:

- **Azure Active Directory:** AVD uses Azure Active Directory, better known as Azure AD, to manage identity and access (IAM). We cover this topic in more detail later in this chapter.

- **Azure Virtual Network:** AVD compute resources use the Azure Virtual Network, better known as a VNet, to communicate privately with other Azure compute resources and between the virtual machines. You can define network topology to access AVD from the Internet or internally, based on your organization's policies. AVD can also be connected to on-premises infrastructure but utilizing a virtual private network (VPN) or an Express Route connection.

- **Active Directory Domain Services (AD DS):** It is a requirement for AVD virtual machines to be domain-joined, so there must be a domain controller that is accessible in your network. AD DS must have a sync with Azure AD that will allow for a Single Sign-On (SSO) experience to be used to access the AVD services. The Azure AD connect service is utilized to synchronize on-premises identity objects with Azure AD.

- **AVD Session Hosts:** Session hosts are the virtual machines in a hostpool, which can run any of the following operating systems:

  - Windows Server 2012 R2 and above

  - Windows 7 Enterprise

  - Windows 10 Enterprise

- Windows 10 Enterprise Multi-session

- Custom image with pre-loaded configuration

You can customize the VM size, which includes the amount of virtual CPU, better known as vCPU, memory (RAM), and GPU-enabled virtual machines. Every session host will have an AVD host agent installed by default, which will register the session host into the workspace/tenant.

- **AVD Workspace:** Also known as the AVD tenant, this is the service that manages the session hosts and publishes the hostpool resources.

From a BCP perspective, you should also include the following components, which are managed by the consumer and are included in any sort of BCP plan:

- **Master VM Images:** When provisioning hostpools you need to provide a mast image, which can either be one you customized and uploaded or one from the Azure image library. These are important when you are setting up new hostpools, so they are vital in a BCP plan.

- **FSLogix:** As discussed in Chapter 2, FSLogix is the component that allows users logon profiles to roam between the different session hosts. This is a critical component for AVD, as the profile needs to be accessible whenever a user logs in to the environment.

- **MSIX App Attach:** As discussed in Chapter 5, MSIX App Attach allows you to store application images away from the operating system (OS). This is not a standard component, but if you have used it to provision applications via a RemoteApp, then it is vital.

This section looked at the elements and components of AVD that you need to include in a BCP plan. The next section discusses the different options and features that you can utilize in Azure to facilitate business continuity with AVD.

Azure BCP Options for Azure Virtual Desktop

Azure has multiple services and features that allow you to make your AVD environment more resilient. You can incorporate these services and features in your BCP plan when designing it.

Availability Sets

This is a logical grouping service that isolates virtual machines that are added to it from one another when they are deployed within a region. An availability set consists of two elements (see Figure 6-1):

- **Update domains:** These ensure that a subset of your virtual machines remains available during maintenance windows.

- **Fault domains (FDs):** These signify the physical areas of the Azure Data Centers and ensure there is a physical segregation between physical racks that host virtual machines in the data centers.

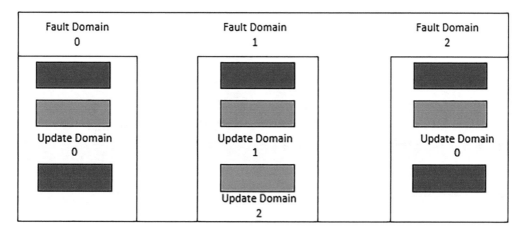

Figure 6-1. *Example of fault domains and update domains*

Availability sets can be a main option for resiliency for AVD hostpools when you are utilizing an Azure VM for a domain controller.

Availability Zones

Availability zones (see Figure 6-2) are individual physical locations that sit within a specific region. They have their own cooling, power, and networking segregated from other locations. Availability zones allow you protect against data center disasters but still utilize specific regions. For example, virtual machines resources are *zonal services* that you can deploy to certain zones in a region. There are some services, however, known as *zone-redundant services*, that can replicate across availability zones in a certain region. Both these services ensure that there is no single point of failure in an Azure region.

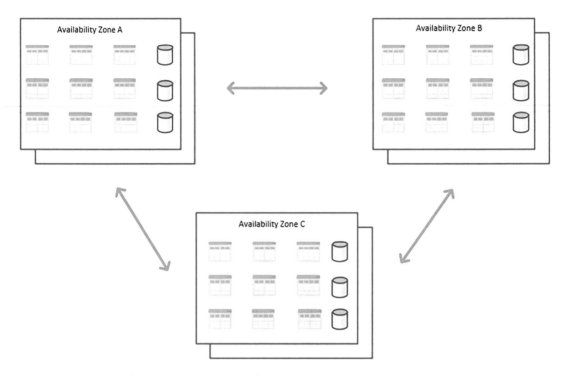

Figure 6-2. *Availability zone example*

Region Pairing

Region pairing symbolizes a group of data centers that function inside a latency-defined boundary and are attached to a dedicated, regional low-latency network. Every Azure region has another region that it is paired with and they are never updated at the same time. They are always updated separately. It is essential to utilize region pairing in your BCP plan and take advantage of its features.

Azure Site Recovery

Azure Site Recovery, also known as ASR, is the Azure native service that manages disaster recovery by replicating virtual machines between Azure regions. ARS will start the failover process to a different session host in another region if the primary zone is having issues.

ASR allows you to replicate domain controllers, session host virtual machines, and data throughout regions to a second region. You can also use automation scripts to failover resources that are not virtual machines and Azure Storage.

You can define the retention point history and the frequency of snapshots by using the customizable replication policies in ASR. The snapshot of a virtual machine allows you to create a recovery point. There are two types of snapshots:

- **Crash-consistent recovery:** This is the default for capturing snapshots in five-minute intervals and symbolizes the content that's on the disks at the time the snapshot is taken.

- **App-consistent recovery:** This encapsulates all the same content as crash-consistent recovery as well as all the in-memory data and in-process transactions.

Azure Backup

Azure Backup is the native backup service in Azure that enables you to back up other Azure native services. It utilizes no infrastructure solutions that allows self-service backups and restores. You can utilize this service to preserve copies of stateful data that enables you to recover older data.

This section discussed the services in Azure that can be included in your BCP plan. The next section takes a closer look at DR objectives and metrics.

DR Objectives and Metrics

There are various objectives and metrics you need to understand and include as part of your BCP/DR services. They include:

- **Recovery point objective (RPO):** This is the least possible amount of content that you must provide back to the end client for service, based on the assets that are backed up and deemed to be recovered.

- **Recovery time objective (RTO):** This is essentially a measurement of the amount of downtime or outage an organization can afford to have. It is the most amount of time you are allowed to have to complete the restoration process.

- **Retention period:** This is the longest amount of time you retain a backup set before it needs to be replaced.

This section was a short look at disaster recovery objectives and metrics. You will now complete a few lab exercises to configure a backup of a virtual machine session host and then complete an exercise lab to restore a VM.

Back Up a Session Host with Azure Backup

1. Log in to the Azure Portal at https://portal.azure.com.

2. In the top search bar, type **Virtual Machines** and select the relevant option, as shown in Figure 6-3.

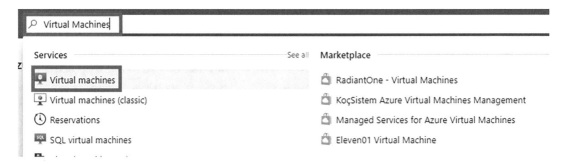

Figure 6-3. *Search for the virtual machine service*

3. Click the virtual machine you want to back up. Then in the left menu, navigate to Operations ➤ Backup, as shown in Figure 6-4.

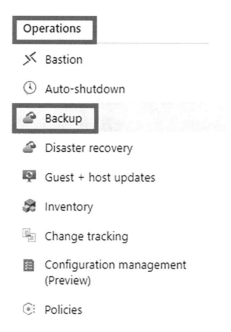

Figure 6-4. *Navigate to Azure Backup operations for the VM*

4. In the middle pane, you can customize the following options (see
    Figure 6-5). Click Enable when you're done:

    - **Recovery Services Vault:** This holds the backup copies you can
      monitor using this vault.

    - **Resource Group:** Specify the resource group where you want to
      store this recovery vault.

    - **Choose Backup Policy:** This specifies the frequency and time at
      which items will be backed up and how long the backup copies
      are retained.

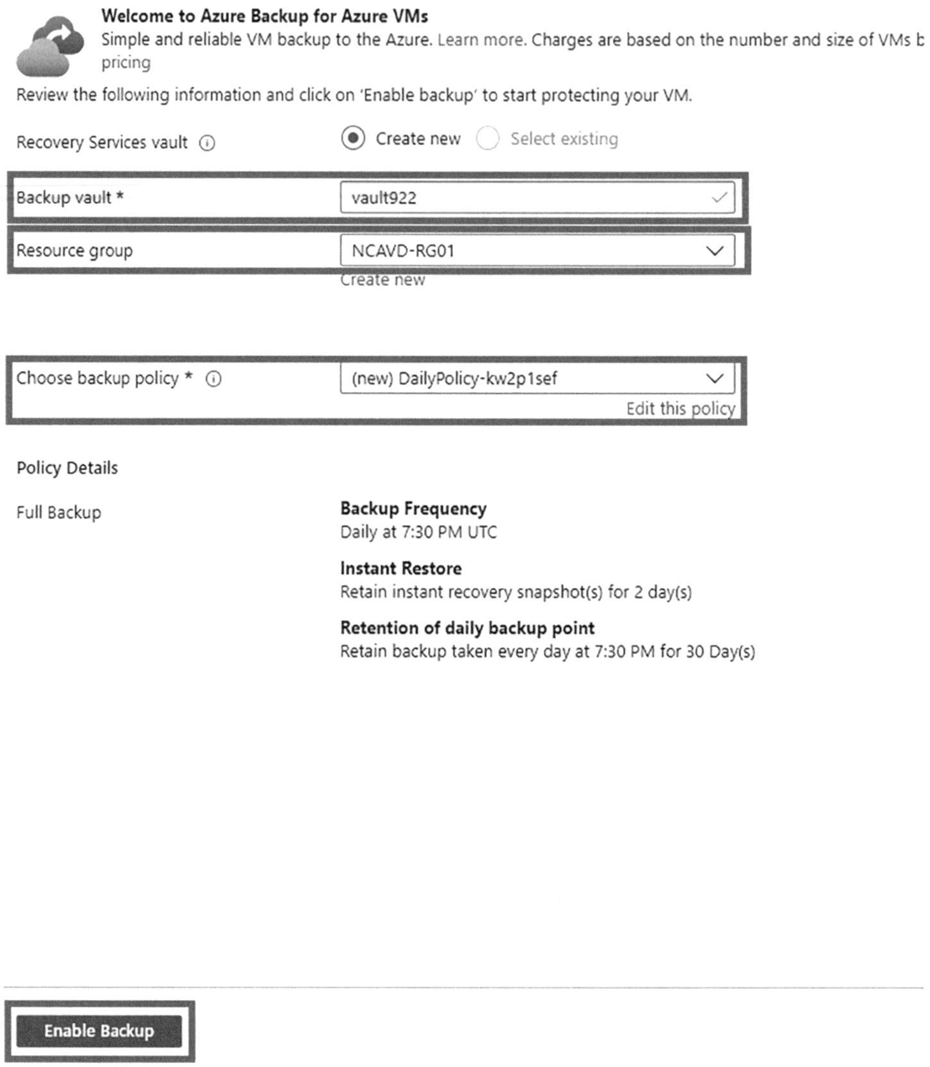

Welcome to Azure Backup for Azure VMs
Simple and reliable VM backup to the Azure. Learn more. Charges are based on the number and size of VMs b
pricing

Review the following information and click on 'Enable backup' to start protecting your VM.

Recovery Services vault ⓘ   ⦿ Create new   ◯ Select existing

Backup vault *	vault922	✓
Resource group	NCAVD-RG01	∨

Create new

Choose backup policy * ⓘ	(new) DailyPolicy-kw2p1sef	∨
		Edit this policy

Policy Details

Full Backup

Backup Frequency
Daily at 7:30 PM UTC

Instant Restore
Retain instant recovery snapshot(s) for 2 day(s)

Retention of daily backup point
Retain backup taken every day at 7:30 PM for 30 Day(s)

Enable Backup

Figure 6-5. *Configure and enable the backup of the VM*

The backup will take several minutes to process and set up. Once the deployment finishes, you will start to see restore points appear over the next few days (see Figure 6-6).

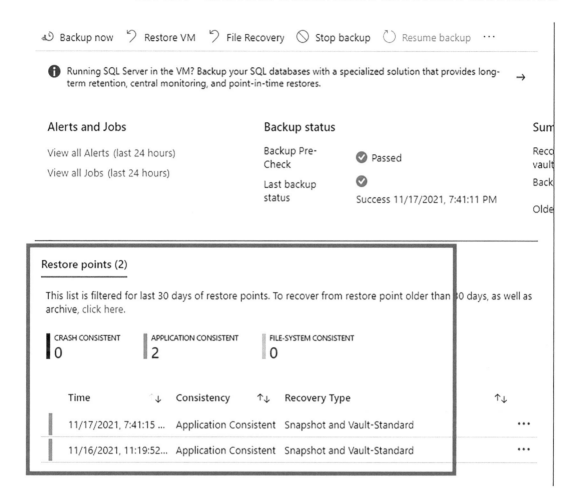

Figure 6-6. *Azure Backup restore points*

Restore a VM

You can now complete a lab to restore the backed up VM:

1. On the backup page for the VM, click Restore VM if you want to restore the entire VM or click File Recovery if you want to restore specific files from the VM. In this example, we restore the VM. See Figure 6-7.

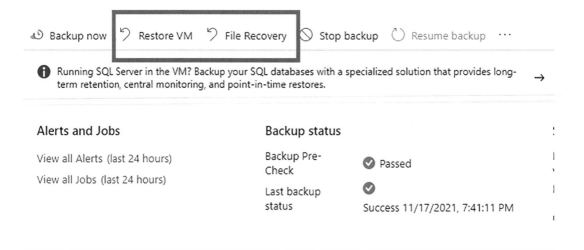

Figure 6-7. *Restore a VM or file recovery*

2. On the Restore Virtual Machine page, select the restore point you want to restore from, as shown in Figures 6-8 and 6-9.

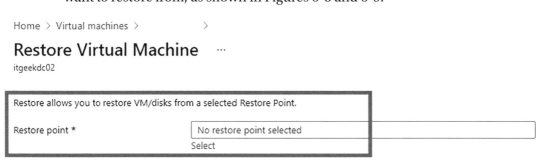

Figure 6-8. *Click restore point*

Select restore point

Start Date	End Date	Recovery point consistency
11/04/2021	11/18/2021	All restore points

█ CRASH CONSISTENT   █ APPLICATION CONSISTENT   █ FILE-SYSTEM CONSISTENT

Time	Consistency	Recovery Type
11/17/2021, 7:41:15 PM	Application Consistent	Snapshot and Vault-Standard
11/16/2021, 11:19:52 PM	Application Consistent	Snapshot and Vault-Standard

Figure 6-9. *Select the relevant restore point*

3. After you select the relevant restore point, complete the following settings:

- **Restore Type:** Restore a VM creates a new virtual machine and does not override the backed up VM. To restore a special network configuration, use Restore Disks. Restore Disks will create new disks in the selected storage account.

- **Virtual Machine Name:** The name of the to-be-restored virtual machine.

- **Resource Group:** Enter the resource group you want to restore the new VM to.

- **Virtual Network:** Enter the virtual network you want to restore the new VM to.

- **Subnet:** Enter the subnet in the virtual machine you want to restore the new VM to.

- **Staging Location:** It is strongly recommended that you create a new storage account and select it here for restoring premium VMs.

4. Click Restore and allow this process to complete.

In this section you completed two lab exercises to back up an Azure VM and then restore an Azure VM. The next section takes a closer look at automating Azure Virtual Desktop Management tasks.

Automating Azure Virtual Desktop Management Tasks

Azure Virtual Desktop is a cloud hosted, managed service provided by Microsoft that allows you to utilize a Microsoft control plane. When you have fully deployed the platform and all its integrated services, you then need to understand the most efficient way of managing the service. Automating management tasks in your cloud environment, including Azure Virtual Desktop, decreases your administrative overhead and allows you to provide a much better experience to your end users. This section looks at scaling session hosts using Azure automation.

You can minimize your Azure Virtual Desktop implementation expense by scaling your VMs. This is the process of powering down and stopping (deallocating) the VMs when your organization has off-peak times and then ensuring they are switched batch on before your organization's working hours start. You can use the Azure Automation scaling tool to:

- Schedule VMs to start and stop based on peak and off-peak business hours

- Scale out VMs based on the number of sessions per CPU core

- Scale in VMs during off-peak hours, leaving the minimum number of session host VMs running

It is important to understand this tool's limitations as well as its benefits:

- Only pooled multi-session session VMs are supported, not personal VMs.

- You can only use Azure Automation with resources that are in the same subscription.

- If the process of stopping and starting a VM takes longer than three hours, the job will fail. This is because an automation runbook has a maximum runtime of three hours.

- CPU or memory-based scaling is not supported with Azure Automation.

- One of the VMs needs to be turned on for the Azure Automation tool to work.

You are now going to do a lab exercise to implement the Azure Automation services. You need to have the following prerequisites in place before you can start this exercise:

- An AVD hostpool

- Virtual machines that are configured and registered with the AVD service

- An administrator account with at least Contributor access to the entire subscription

- The client you are completing the lab from has Windows PowerShell 5.1 or later installed

The first step is to create an Azure Automation account:

1. Open Windows PowerShell and run the cmdlet shown in Figure 6-10. You will be prompted to enter your Microsoft 365 administrator account details.

Figure 6-10. *Login-AzAccount cmdlet*

2. Run the cmdlets shown in Figures 6-11 through to Figure 6-14. These will download the script for creating the Azure Automation account.

```
PS C:\WINDOWS\system32> New-Item -ItemType Directory -Path "C:\Temp" -Force


    Directory: C:\


Mode                 LastWriteTime         Length Name
----                 -------------         ------ ----
d-----       18-11-2021     15:15                 Temp
```

Figure 6-11. *Create a temp folder on the C drive*

The command in Figure 6-11 creates a temp folder on the C drive, which will be where we download the script.

```
PS C:\WINDOWS\system32> Set-Location -Path "C:\Temp"
```

Figure 6-12. *Set the default folder location*

The command in Figure 6-12 sets the temp folder on the C drive to the default download location.

```
PS C:\Temp> $Uri = "https://raw.githubusercontent.com/Azure/RDS-Templates
/master/wvd-templates/wvd-scaling-script/CreateOrUpdateAzAutoAccount.ps1"
```

Figure 6-13. *Set the URL to download the script from*

The command in Figure 6-13 sets the URL from which you will download the script.

```
PS C:\Temp> Invoke-WebRequest -Uri $Uri -OutFile ".\CreateOrUpdateAzAutoAccount.ps1"
```

Figure 6-14. *cmdlet to download the PowerShell script*

The command in Figure 6-14 downloads the required script from the stored URL into the temp folder.

3. The script shown in Figure 6-15 creates the Azure Automation account. In this case I have left the values, but you can specify the Azure AD Tenant ID, Azure Subscription, Resource Group, Automation Account Name, Location, and Log Analytics Workspace Name in this script as you prefer.

```
PS C:\Temp> $Uri = "https://raw.githubusercontent.com/Azure/RDS-Templates/master/wvd-templates/
wvd-scaling-script/CreateOrUpdateAzAutoAccount.ps1"
PS C:\Temp> Invoke-WebRequest -Uri $Uri -OutFile ".\CreateOrUpdateAzAutoAccount.ps1"
PS C:\Temp> $Params = @{
>>      "AADTenantId"           = "<Azure_Active_Directory_tenant_ID>"   # Optional. If not spe
cified, it will use the current Azure context
>>      "SubscriptionId"        = "<Azure_subscription_ID>"              # Optional. If not spe
cified, it will use the current Azure context
>>      "UseARMAPI"             = $true
>>      "ResourceGroupName"     = "<Resource_group_name>"               # Optional. Default: "
WVDAutoScaleResourceGroup"
>>      "AutomationAccountName" = "<Automation_account_name>"           # Optional. Default: "
WVDAutoScaleAutomationAccount"
>>      "Location"              = "<Azure_region_for_deployment>"
>>      "WorkspaceName"         = "<Log_analytics_workspace_name>"       # Optional. If specifi
ed, Log Analytics will be used to configure the custom log table that the runbook PowerShell sc
ript can send logs to
>> }
PS C:\Temp>
PS C:\Temp> .\CreateOrUpdateAzAutoAccount.ps1 @Params
```

Figure 6-15. *Create the Automation account script*

Once the Azure Automation script has completed, you will find the new automation account in the Azure Portal. You now need to create the Run as Accounts option for Azure Automation.

4. Log in to the Azure Portal with a global admin account at https://portal.azure.com.

5. In the top search box, type **Automation Accounts** and select the relevant option, as shown in Figure 6-16.

Figure 6-16. *Navigate to Automation Accounts*

6. Select the name of your Azure Automation account, as shown in Figure 6-17.

Home >

Automation Accounts ⚲ ⋯
IamITGeek (iamitgeek.com)

+ Create   ⚙ Manage view ∨   ↻ Refresh   ↓ Export to CSV   ⤴ Open query | ⊘ Assign tags | ⚐ Feedback

| Filter for any field... | Subscription == **Iamitgeek** | Resource group == **all** ✕ | Location == **all** ✕ | ⁺⛛ Add filter |

Showing 1 to 1 of 1 records.

☐ Name ↑	Type ↑↓	Resource group
☐ ⚙ AZ-140AA	Automation Account	ITGEEKRG01

Figure 6-17. *Select the Azure Automation account you created earlier*

7. On the left-side pane, navigate to Account Settings and select Run
    as Accounts, as shown in Figure 6-18.

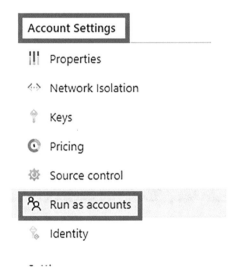

Figure 6-18. *Navigate to Run as Accounts*

8. Click + Azure Run As Account, as shown in Figure 6-19.

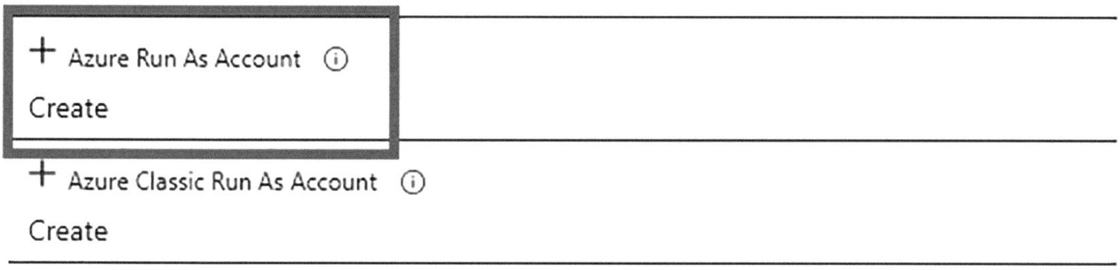

+ Azure Run As Account ⓘ

Create

+ Azure Classic Run As Account ⓘ

Create

Figure 6-19. *Azure Run As Account*

9. Click the Create button at the bottom-left side of the window to start the process.

10. Once this process is completed, you will find a resource called *AzureRunAsConnection* in the specific automation account.

    Now that you have created the Azure Automation account and the run as account, you need to create the Azure LogicApp and execution schedule:

11. Run PowerShell with administrator rights and then run the Login-AZAccount cmdlet.

12. If you have not completed Steps 2 and 3, do so now.

13. Run the cmdlet in Figure 6-20 to set the URL you will download the script from.

```
PS C:\Temp> $Uri = "https://raw.githubusercontent.com/Azure/RDS-Temp
lates/master/wvd-templates/wvd-scaling-script/CreateOrUpdateAzLogicA
pp.ps1"
```

Figure 6-20. *Set the URL from where you will download the script*

14. Run the cmdlet in Figure 6-21 to download the script.

```
PS C:\Temp> Invoke-WebRequest -Uri $Uri -OutFile ".\CreateOrUpdateAz
LogicApp.ps1"
```

Figure 6-21. *Download the LogicApp script*

15. Run the following script for each virtual machine hostpool you want to autoscale.

```
$AADTenantId = (Get-AzContext).Tenant.Id

$AzSubscription = Get-AzSubscription | Out-GridView -OutputMode:Single
-Title "Select your Azure Subscription"
Select-AzSubscription -Subscription $AzSubscription.Id

$ResourceGroup = Get-AzResourceGroup | Out-GridView -OutputMode:Single
-Title "Select the resource group for the new Azure Logic App"

$WVDHostPool = Get-AzResource -ResourceType "Microsoft.
DesktopVirtualization/hostpools" | Out-GridView -OutputMode:Single -Title
"Select the host pool you'd like to scale"

$LogAnalyticsWorkspaceId = Read-Host -Prompt "If you want to use Log
Analytics, enter the Log Analytics Workspace ID returned by when you
created the Azure Automation account, otherwise leave it blank"
$LogAnalyticsPrimaryKey = Read-Host -Prompt "If you want to use Log
Analytics, enter the Log Analytics Primary Key returned by when you created
the Azure Automation account, otherwise leave it blank"
$RecurrenceInterval = Read-Host -Prompt "Enter how often you'd like the job
to run in minutes, e.g. '15'"
$BeginPeakTime = Read-Host -Prompt "Enter the start time for peak hours
in local time, e.g. 9:00"
$EndPeakTime = Read-Host -Prompt "Enter the end time for peak hours
in local time, e.g. 18:00"
$TimeDifference = Read-Host -Prompt "Enter the time difference between
local time and UTC in hours, e.g. +5:30"
$SessionThresholdPerCPU = Read-Host -Prompt "Enter the maximum number of
sessions per CPU that will be used as a threshold to determine when new
session host VMs need to be started during peak hours"
$MinimumNumberOfRDSH = Read-Host -Prompt "Enter the minimum number of
session host VMs to keep running during off-peak hours"
$MaintenanceTagName = Read-Host -Prompt "Enter the name of the Tag
associated with VMs you don't want to be managed by this scaling tool"
```

```
$LimitSecondsToForceLogOffUser = Read-Host -Prompt "Enter the number of
seconds to wait before automatically signing out users. If set to 0, any
session host VM that has user sessions, will be left untouched"
$LogOffMessageTitle = Read-Host -Prompt "Enter the title of the message
sent to the user before they are forced to sign out"
$LogOffMessageBody = Read-Host -Prompt "Enter the body of the message sent
to the user before they are forced to sign out"

$AutoAccount = Get-AzAutomationAccount | Out-GridView -OutputMode:Single
-Title "Select the Azure Automation account"
$AutoAccountConnection = Get-AzAutomationConnection -ResourceGroupName
$AutoAccount.ResourceGroupName -AutomationAccountName $AutoAccount.
AutomationAccountName | Out-GridView -OutputMode:Single -Title "Select the
Azure RunAs connection asset"

$WebhookURIAutoVar = Get-AzAutomationVariable -Name 'WebhookURIARMBased'
-ResourceGroupName $AutoAccount.ResourceGroupName -AutomationAccountName
$AutoAccount.AutomationAccountName

$Params = @{
    "AADTenantId"                    =
$AADTenantId                         # Optional. If not specified, it
will use the current Azure context
    "SubscriptionID"                 = $AzSubscription.
Id                      # Optional. If not specified, it will use the
current Azure context
    "ResourceGroupName"              = $ResourceGroup.
ResourceGroupName       # Optional. Default: "WVDAutoScaleResourceGroup"
    "Location"                       = $ResourceGroup.
Location                # Optional. Default: "West US2"
    "UseARMAPI"                      = $true
    "HostPoolName"                   = $WVDHostPool.Name
    "HostPoolResourceGroupName"      = $WVDHostPool.
ResourceGroupName           # Optional. Default: same as ResourceGroupName
param value
```

```
    "LogAnalyticsWorkspaceId"        =
$LogAnalyticsWorkspaceId                 # Optional. If not specified,
script will not log to the Log Analytics
    "LogAnalyticsPrimaryKey"         =
$LogAnalyticsPrimaryKey                  # Optional. If not specified,
script will not log to the Log Analytics
    "ConnectionAssetName"            = $AutoAccountConnection.
Name              # Optional. Default: "AzureRunAsConnection"
    "RecurrenceInterval"             =
$RecurrenceInterval                      # Optional. Default: 15
    "BeginPeakTime"                  =
$BeginPeakTime                           # Optional. Default: "09:00"
    "EndPeakTime"                    =
$EndPeakTime                             # Optional. Default: "17:00"
    "TimeDifference"                 =
$TimeDifference                          # Optional. Default: "-7:00"
    "SessionThresholdPerCPU"         =
$SessionThresholdPerCPU                  # Optional. Default: 1
    "MinimumNumberOfRDSH"            =
$MinimumNumberOfRDSH                     # Optional. Default: 1
    "MaintenanceTagName"             =
$MaintenanceTagName                      # Optional.
    "LimitSecondsToForceLogOffUser" =
$LimitSecondsToForceLogOffUser           # Optional. Default: 1
    "LogOffMessageTitle"             =
$LogOffMessageTitle                      # Optional. Default: "Machine is
about to shutdown."
    "LogOffMessageBody"              =
$LogOffMessageBody                       # Optional. Default: "Your session
will be logged off. Please save and close everything."
    "WebhookURI"                     = $WebhookURIAutoVar.Value
}

.\CreateOrUpdateAzLogicApp.ps1 @Params
```

Once you run the script, your Azure LogicApp will appear in the resource group and you can start to manage the scaling tool.

In this section you completed a lab exercise on how to create an Azure Automation account when you want to use automation with your Azure Virtual Desktop resources to manage them. The next section looks at using autoscaling with your Azure Virtual Desktop hostpools.

Using Autoscale for Azure Virtual Desktop Hostpools

You can utilize the autoscale feature with Azure Virtual Desktop to scale up or down and save costs.

Autoscaling plans can be created that are based on:

- Time of day

- Session limits per session host

- Specific days of the week

There are specific requirements that need to be met before you look at creating your first scaling plan:

- Only pooled hostpools are supported with scaling plans.

- You need to have a MaxSessionLimit configured on all hostpools you want to utilize autoscaling with.

- Azure Virtual Desktop must have the relevant access to power on virtual machine compute resources.

We are going to start by creating a custom RBAC role in the subscription. This will enable Azure Virtual Desktop to manage power for all the VMs.

1. You can use the following JSON template to create the custom role, as it has all the permissions settings you need:

```
{
 "properties": {
 "roleName": "Autoscale",
 "description": "Friendly description.",
 "assignableScopes": [
 "/subscriptions/<SubscriptionID>"
```

```
    ],
    "permissions": [
     {
     "actions": [
                        "Microsoft.Insights/eventtypes/values/read",
                        "Microsoft.Compute/virtualMachines/deallocate/
                        action",
                        "Microsoft.Compute/virtualMachines/restart/
                        action",
                        "Microsoft.Compute/virtualMachines/powerOff/
                        action",
                        "Microsoft.Compute/virtualMachines/start/action",
                        "Microsoft.Compute/virtualMachines/read",
                        "Microsoft.DesktopVirtualization/hostpools/read",
                        "Microsoft.DesktopVirtualization/
                        hostpools/write",
                        "Microsoft.DesktopVirtualization/hostpools/
                        sessionhosts/read",
                        "Microsoft.DesktopVirtualization/hostpools/
                        sessionhosts/write",
                        "Microsoft.DesktopVirtualization/hostpools/
                        sessionhosts/usersessions/delete",
                        "Microsoft.DesktopVirtualization/hostpools/
                        sessionhosts/usersessions/read",
                        "Microsoft.DesktopVirtualization/hostpools/
                        sessionhosts/usersessions/sendMessage/action",
                        "Microsoft.DesktopVirtualization/hostpools/
                        sessionhosts/usersessions/read"
    ],
      "notActions": [],
      "dataActions": [],
      "notDataActions": []
     }
    ]
   }
  }
```

Once the custom role has been created, you need to assign the custom roles from the Azure Portal.

2. Open the Azure Portal at `https://portal.azure.com` and navigate to Subscriptions.

3. On the left-side pane, go to Access Control (IAM), as shown in Figure 6-22.

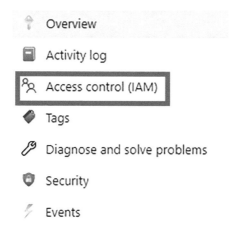

Figure 6-22. *Access control within the subscription service*

4. Click the + Add button and select Add Custom Role, as shown in Figure 6-23.

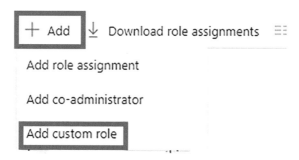

Figure 6-23. *Add a custom role*

5. Enter a custom name and click Next.

6. On the Permissions tab, add the permissions for Microsoft. DesktopVirtualization, as shown in Figure 6-24.

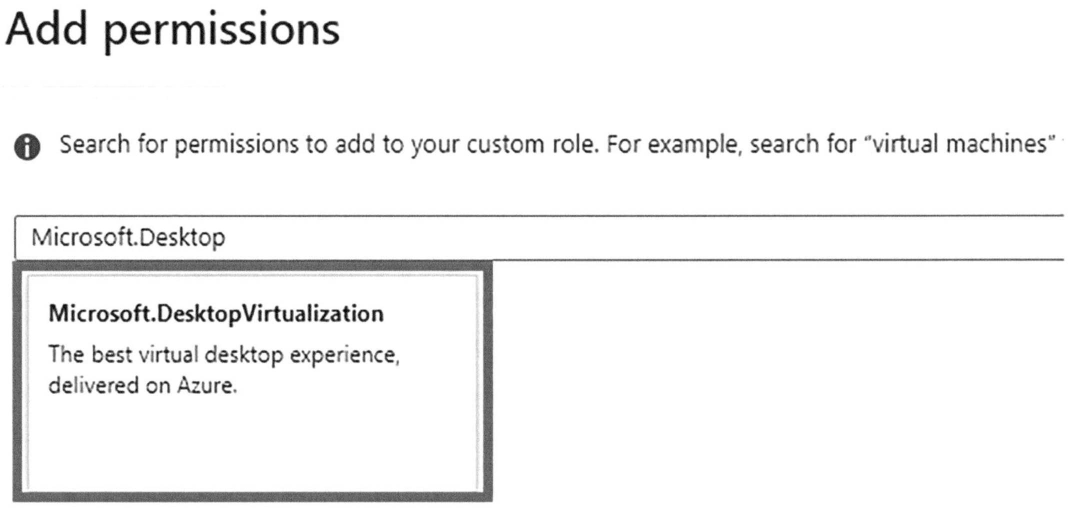

Add permissions

ⓘ Search for permissions to add to your custom role. For example, search for "virtual machines"

Microsoft.Desktop

Microsoft.DesktopVirtualization
The best virtual desktop experience, delivered on Azure.

Figure 6-24. *Add permissions for Microsoft.DesktopVirtualization*

7. On the Microsoft.DesktopVirtualization permissions page, add the following permissions:

```
"Microsoft.DesktopVirtualization/hostpools/sessionhosts/read"
"Microsoft.DesktopVirtualization/hostpools/sessionhosts/write"
"Microsoft.DesktopVirtualization/hostpools/sessionhosts/
usersessions/delete"
"Microsoft.DesktopVirtualization/hostpools/sessionhosts/
usersessions/read"
"Microsoft.DesktopVirtualization/hostpools/sessionhosts/
usersessions/sendMessage/action"
"Microsoft.DesktopVirtualization/hostpools/sessionhosts/
usersessions/read"
```

8. Add the following Microsoft.Compute permissions:

```
"Microsoft.Insights/eventtypes/values/read"
"Microsoft.Compute/virtualMachines/deallocate/action"
"Microsoft.Compute/virtualMachines/restart/action"
"Microsoft.Compute/virtualMachines/powerOff/action"
```

```
"Microsoft.Compute/virtualMachines/start/action"
"Microsoft.Compute/virtualMachines/read"
```

Once you have added these permissions, you can create the custom role. You are now ready to create the scaling plan.

9.   Navigate to Azure Virtual Desktop ➤ Scaling Plans, as shown in Figure 6-25.

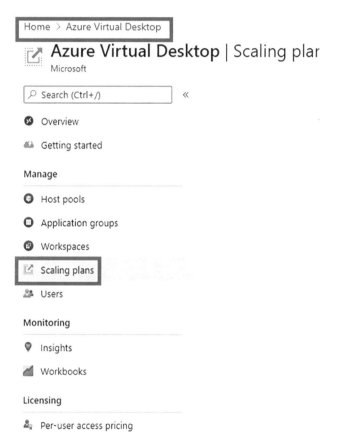

Figure 6-25. *Scaling plans*

10.   Click + Create, as shown in Figure 6-26.

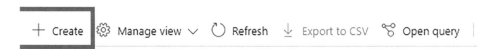

Figure 6-26.   *Create scaling plan button*

11.   Complete the Basics tab with the following settings (see
      Figure 6-27). When you're done, click Next:

  • Subscription

  • Resource Group

  • Scaling Plan Name

  • Location

  • Description (Optional)

  • Time Zone

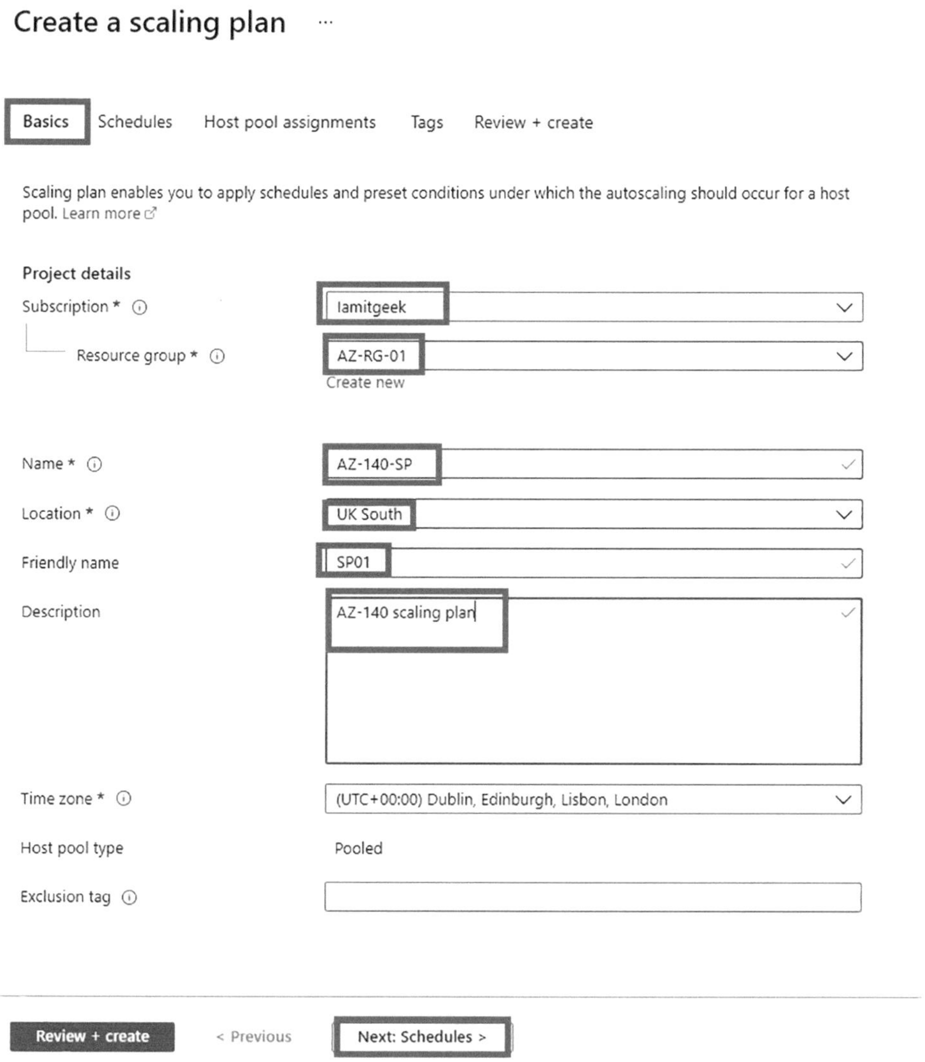

Create a scaling plan   ⋯

Basics   Schedules   Host pool assignments   Tags   Review + create

Scaling plan enables you to apply schedules and preset conditions under which the autoscaling should occur for a host pool. Learn more ⬚

Project details

Subscription * ⓘ

Iamitgeek

Resource group * ⓘ

AZ-RG-01

Create new

Name * ⓘ

AZ-140-SP

Location * ⓘ

UK South

Friendly name

SP01

Description

AZ-140 scaling plan

Time zone * ⓘ

(UTC+00:00) Dublin, Edinburgh, Lisbon, London

Host pool type

Pooled

Exclusion tag ⓘ

Review + create   < Previous   Next: Schedules >

Figure 6-27. *Basic tab of scaling plan*

12.   Click + Add Schedule, as shown in Figure 6-28.

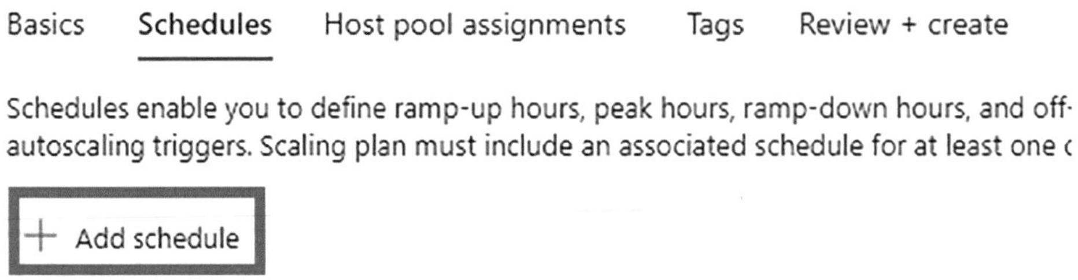

Basics   **Schedules**   Host pool assignments   Tags   Review + create

Schedules enable you to define ramp-up hours, peak hours, ramp-down hours, and off-autoscaling triggers. Scaling plan must include an associated schedule for at least one (

+ Add schedule

Figure 6-28. *Create a schedule*

13. Complete the following settings on the Add Schedule ➤ General
     tab and click Next (see Figure 6-29):

     • Schedule Name

     • Repeat On (choose the days you want to repeat the schedule on)

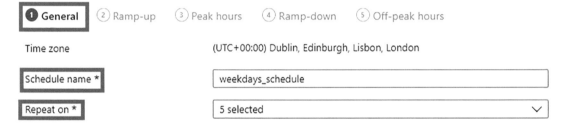

Figure 6-29. *Add the schedule settings*

14. Complete the following settings on the Add Schedule ➤ Ramp-up
     tab and click Next (see Figure 6-30):

     • Start time (24-hour system)

     • Load balancing algorithm

     • Minimum percentage of hosts

     • Capacity threshold

Add a schedule

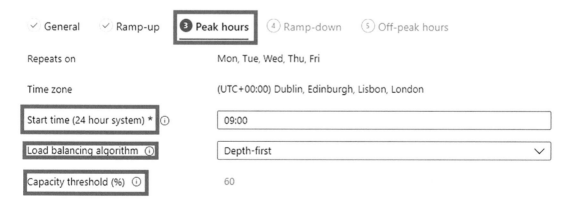

General   **2 Ramp-up**   ③ Peak hours   ④ Ramp-down   ⑤ Off-peak hours

Repeats on	Mon, Tue, Wed, Thu, Fri
Time zone	(UTC+00:00) Dublin, Edinburgh, Lisbon, London
Start time (24 hour system) * ⓘ	08:00
Load balancing algorithm ⓘ	Breadth-first
Minimum percentage of hosts (%) * ⓘ	20
Capacity threshold (%) * ⓘ	60

Figure 6-30. *Complete the ramp-up settings*

15.   Complete the following settings on the Add Schedule ➤ Peak
hours tab and click Next (see Figure 6-31):

- Start time (24-hour system)

- Load Balancing algorithm

- Capacity threshold

General   ✓ Ramp-up   **3 Peak hours**   ④ Ramp-down   ⑤ Off-peak hours

Repeats on	Mon, Tue, Wed, Thu, Fri
Time zone	(UTC+00:00) Dublin, Edinburgh, Lisbon, London
Start time (24 hour system) * ⓘ	09:00
Load balancing algorithm ⓘ	Depth-first
Capacity threshold (%) ⓘ	60

Figure 6-31. *Complete the Peak Hours settings*

16.   Complete the following settings on the Add Schedule ➤
      Ramp-down tab and click Next (see Figure 6-32):

- Start time (24-hour system)

- Load balancing algorithm

- Minimum percentage of hosts

- Capacity threshold

- Force logoff users

- Delay time before logging out users and shutting
  down VMs (min)

- Notification message

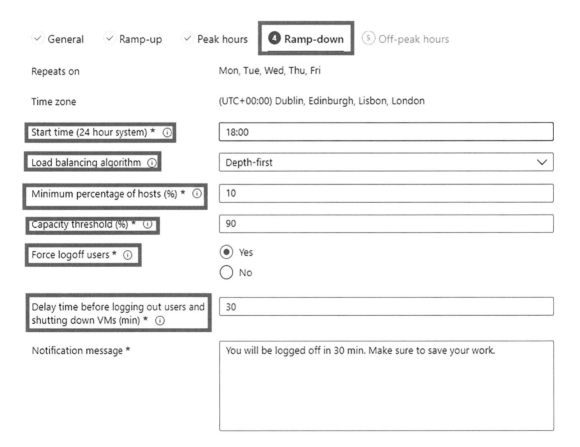

Figure 6-32. Complete the ramp-down settings

17. Complete these settings on the Add Schedule ➤ Off-Peak Hours
    tab (see Figure 6-33). Click Add and then Next.

    - Start time (24-hour system)

    - Load balancing algorithm

    - Capacity threshold

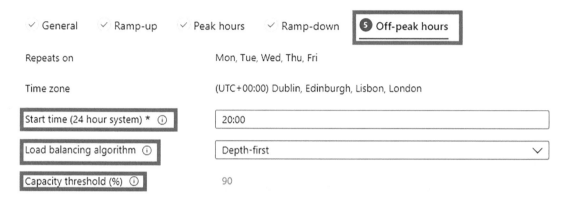

Figure 6-33. Completethe off-peak hours settings

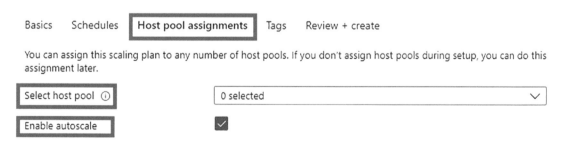

Figure 6-34. Hostpool assignment settings

18. On the Host Pool Assignments tab, enter the settings shown in
    Figure 6-34 and click Next.

19. Enter a tag, then click Review + Create.

This section configured a scaling plan for Azure Virtual Desktop hostpools. The next section moves onto monitoring and managing performance and health in Azure Virtual Desktop.

Monitoring and Managing Performance and Health

An important aspect of any infrastructure hosted in the cloud is ensuring you have a robust management solution in place to monitor health and performance. Azure has native services that can integrate with Azure Virtual Desktop that allow you to monitor the environment efficiently.

This section discusses how you can use Azure Monitor integration with Azure Virtual Desktop and complete a lab exercise to set this up. Azure Monitor includes a dashboard, which is developed on Azure Monitor workbooks and allows support teams to gain further insights into the Azure Virtual Desktop environment.

Before you can implement Azure Monitor with Azure Virtual Desktop, you need to ensure the following components are in place:

- You need to enable data collection on the following items in the Log Analytics workspace:

    - Diagnostics from the Azure Virtual Desktop environment

    - Performance counters (recommended) from the Azure Virtual Desktop session hosts

    - Windows event logs (recommended) from the Azure Virtual Desktop session hosts

- An Azure Virtual Desktop environment must be created on the latest version that is compatible with Azure Resource Manager (ARM) templates.

- At a minimum, one Log Analytics workspace must be implemented.

You also need to ensure the account you are using to configure the Azure Monitor integration with Azure Virtual Desktop has the following permissions:

- Azure Subscription read access

- Resource Group read access

- Log Analytics read access

Log Analytics

As highlighted in the requirements, you need at least one Log Analytics workspace to integrate Azure Monitor with Azure Virtual Desktop. You should create a separate workspace for this service that is designated to Azure Virtual Desktop. You can complete the following steps to create a Log Analytics workspace:

1. In the Azure Portal, type **Log Analytics** in the top search bar and select it from the available options, as shown in Figure 6-35.

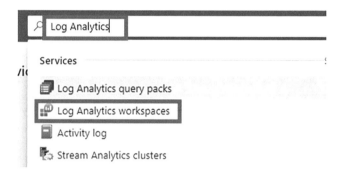

Figure 6-35. *Navigate to the Log Analytics Portal*

2. Click Create.

3. Enter the following details on the Basics tab and click Next when you're done (see Figure 6-36):

   - Subscription

   - Resource Group

   - Name

   - Region

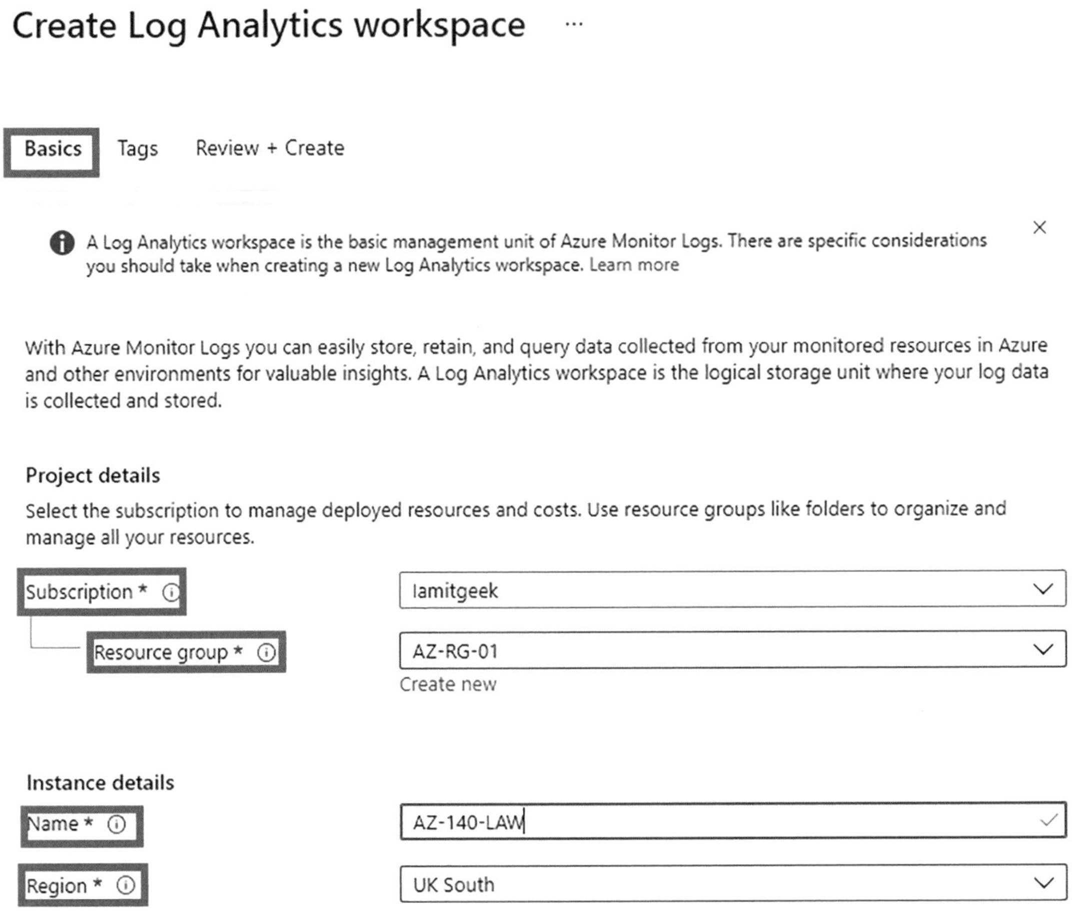

Figure 6-36. *Log Analytics Basic tab*

4.   Enter any relevant tags, then review and create the workspace.

If this is the first time you have accessed Azure Monitor for Azure Virtual Desktop, you need to set up the configuration workbook.

5.   Choose the Azure Virtual Desktop ➤ Insights page and then browse to the bottom of the page and click Configuration Workbook, as shown in Figure 6-37.

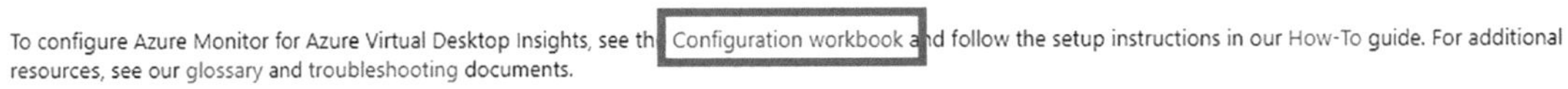

Figure 6-37. *Configuration workbook*

6. Set the Subscription, Resource Group, and the Host Pool settings, as shown in Figure 6-38.

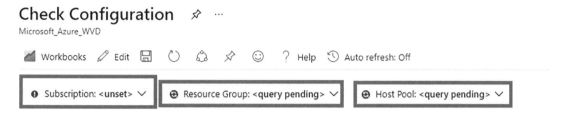

Figure 6-38. *Check the workbook configuration*

Resource Diagnostics

Before you can start to collect information on the Azure Virtual Desktop environment, you need to enable the multiple diagnostics setting in Azure Virtual Desktop. You can set up the Resource Diagnostics settings in the configuration workbook:

1. Under the Resource Diagnostics Settings tab, choose the Log Analytics workspace you set up earlier, as shown in Figure 6-39.

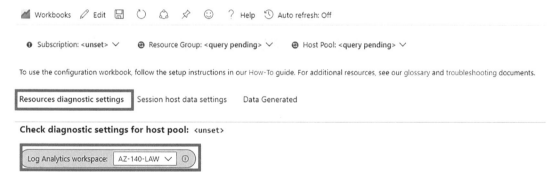

Figure 6-39. *Enable Log Analytics in the workbook*

Hostpool Diagnostics

You can now set up the Hostpool Diagnostic settings by utilizing the Resource Diagnostic settings area in the workbook:

1. Check if the Azure Virtual Desktop diagnostics are enabled under the Hostpool section. If they are not enabled (see Figure 6-40), enable the following diagnostic tables:

- Checkpoint

- Error

- Management

- Connection

- HostRegistration

- AgentHealthStatus

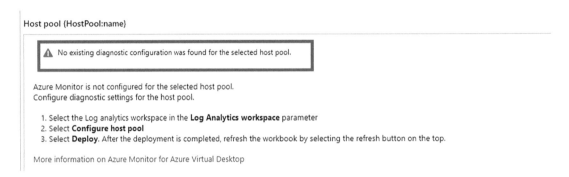

Figure 6-40. *Hostpool diagnostics not enabled*

2. Click Configure Host Pool, as shown in Figure 6-41.

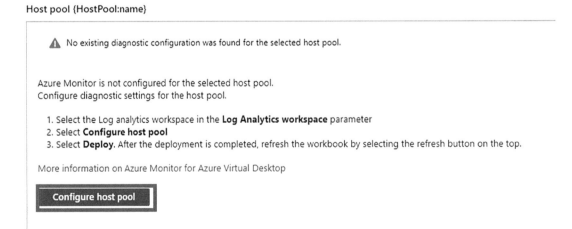

Figure 6-41. *Configure hostpool diagnostics*

3. Review the settings and click Deploy, as shown in Figure 6-42.

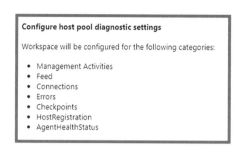

Figure 6-42. *Deploy the hostpool diagnostics settings*

Workspace Diagnostics

You can now set up the Workspace diagnostics in a similar way to how you set up the
hostpool diagnostics:

1. Under Workspace, see if the Azure Virtual Desktop diagnostics are
    enabled. If it is not, you need to enable the following settings:

    • Checkpoint

    • Error

- Management

- Feed

2. Click Configure Workspace.

3. Click Deploy.

Session Host Data Settings

You must install a specific Log Analytics agent on all the Windows session hosts that you want to collect data from. You can create a separate Log Analytics workspace to send session host data to if you want, and this is generally what is recommended.

You need to complete the following steps to set the Log Analytics workspace that will collate the session data:

1. Click the Session Host Data Settings tab in the workbook.

2. Choose the Log Analytics workspace you want to direct the session host data to.

Workspace Performance Counters

If you want to collect performance information from the session hosts, you must enable the specific counters; doing so will start sending the information to the Log Analytics workspace.

Use the following steps to set up performance counters using the configuration workbook:

1. You first need to check Configured Counters under the Workspace Performance Counters to view the counters that are already enabled.

2. Click Configure Performance Counters.

3. Choose Apply Counters.

Windows Event Logs

If you want to collect Windows Event Log errors, warnings, and information, you need to enable this from the session hosts and direct them to the Log Analytics workspace.

Complete the following steps to set up the Windows Event Logs from the configuration workbook:

1. Check the Configured Event Logs under the Windows Event Logs configuration section to see if the event logs have been enabled.

2. Click Configure Events if you find you have missing Windows Event Logs.

3. Click Deploy.

This section looked at Azure Monitor and discussed the different types of information you can gather from Azure Virtual Desktop. The next section looks at Azure Advisor and explains how it integrates with Azure Virtual Desktop.

Utilizing Azure Advisor with Azure Virtual Desktop

Azure Advisor assists end users in fixing common problems on their own, rather than having IT support fix them. Azure Advisor give users recommendations, which then minimizes the number of support requests that are made.

Azure Advisor evaluates your implementation and telemetry and outputs customized recommendations that can help you fix your issues.

To start using Azure Advisor, open the Azure Portal at `https://portal.azure.com` and navigate to the Azure Advisor service. See Figure 6-43.

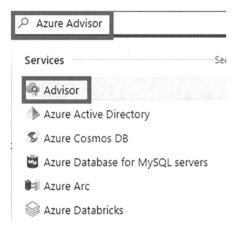

Figure 6-43. *Azure Advisor*

On the Azure Advisor page, you will see five categories:

- Costs

- Security

- Reliability

- Operational Excellence

- Performance

You can click any of these categories, which will then take you to the recommendations for that specific category.

This section was an overview of Azure Advisor and explained how it can recommend various resolutions to help users fix their own issues. You can now move on to the knowledge check to see if you understand the information.

Knowledge Check

The following questions are aimed at testing your understanding of the information in this chapter. It is recommended that you complete all sections and labs in this chapter before attempting these questions.

Check Your Knowledge

1. Which element of an availability set signifies the physical areas of an Azure Data Center and ensures there is physical segregation between the racks?

    *   Update Domains

    *   Fault Domains

    *   Server Racks

2. Which type of Azure Site Recovery disk snapshot is the default option for capturing snapshots in five-minute intervals?

    *   App-consistent recovery

    *   Crash-consistent recovery

3. Which DR objective is a measurement of the amount of downtime or outage a company can afford to have?

    *   Retention period

    *   Recovery point objective (RPO)

    *   Recovery time objective (RTO)

4. Which Azure native tool allows you to automatically manage administrative tasks with your Azure Virtual Desktop environment?

    *   Azure Backup

    *   Azure Automation

    *   Azure Site Recovery

5. Which Azure native service enables you to automatically increase or decrease the number of session hosts in your environment based on specific metrics?

    *   Azure Site Recovery

    *   Autoscale

    *   Azure Monitor

Summary

This chapter looked at planning and implementing business continuity and disaster recovery, automating Azure Virtual Desktop management tasks, and monitoring and managing performance tasks. It is recommended that you complete the labs in this chapter and in the book before taking your exam.

Knowledge Check Answers

Chapter 2 answers:

    1: Web Access, Gateway, and Diagnostics

    2: AVD Workspace, Session Hosts, and Active Directory Domain Services

    3: True

    4: Premium File Shares

    5: Password hash-sync

    6: Microsoft.DesktopVirtualization

Chapter 3 answers:

    1: Personal

    2: Windows 10 Enterprise Multi-Session

    3: Assign the users to the RemoteApp and Desktop Application Groups.

    4: Azure AD DS and Active Directory Domain Services

    5: Capture the Windows VM image

Chapter 4 answers:

    1: Desktop Virtualization Hostpool Reader

    2: Web Access, Diagnostics, and Broker

    3: End User Host Access, Virtual Machine Scaling & Sizing, and Policies for Scaling

    4: Global Admin, Security Administrator, and Conditional Access Administrator

    5: Premium

© Shabaz Darr 2022
S. Darr, *Azure Virtual Desktop Specialist*, https://doi.org/10.1007/978-1-4842-7987-8

Chapter 5 answers:

       1: Azure Page Blobs

       2: Azure Files

       3: Universal Print Connector

Chapter 6 answers:

       1: Fault Domains

       2: Crash-consistent recovery

       3: Recovery time objective (RTO)

       4: Azure Automation

       5: Autoscale

Index

A

Active Directory Domain Services (AD
   DS), 22, 44–46, 77–79, 215
Active Directory Federation Services
   (ADFS), 45
App Container Rule, 202
Application groups, 194
   add, 197
   basics tab, 197
   creation, 196
   feature, 195
   reset settings, 199
   source, 198
   workspace, 199
Application masking, 162, 194, 200–209
Application Rules Editor, 200
Autoscaling plans, 235
   basic tab, 241
   creation, 240
   hostpool assignment settings, 245
   off-peak hours settings, 245
   Peak Hours settings, 243
   ramp-down settings, 244
   ramp-up settings, 243
   schedule settings, 242
Availability sets, 100, 217
Availability zones, 100, 217–218
AzFilesHybrid Azure PowerShell
   module, 77–79
Azure Advisor, 253–254
Azure Automation
   creation, 227

navigation, 229, 230
   scaling tool, 226
   script, 229, 231
   select, 230
Azure Backup, 219
   DR objectives/metrics, 219
   restore VM, 223–225
   session host, 220
   VM, 221, 222
Azure Monitor
   Log Analytics, 247
      Azure Advisor, 253, 254
      basic tab, 248
      Hostpool Diagnostic, 249–251
      navigation, 247
      performance counters, 252
      Resource Diagnostics, 249
      session data, 252
      Windows Event Logs, 253
      Workspace diagnostics, 251
Azure Site Recovery (ASR), 218–219
Azure Storage
   Azure File Sync, 174–177
   cloud endpoint, 178
   server endpoint, 178
   Windows Server, 178
Azure Virtual Desktop (AVD)
   architecture, 19, 20
   assign roles
      admin center, 133, 135, 137
      PowerShell, 137, 138
   Azure Security Center, 155

© Shabaz Darr 2022
S. Darr, *Azure Virtual Desktop Specialist*, https://doi.org/10.1007/978-1-4842-7987-8

Printed in the United States
by Baker & Taylor Publisher Services